How to be a Litigant in Person
In the New Legal World

Revised Edition

MICHAEL LANGFORD

Straightforward Publishing
www.straightforwardbooks.co.uk

Contents

Introduction

"Litigant in Person" is a term used to describe a party in legal proceedings who is conducting their case without legal representation. It could be an individual or a company that acts for itself without lawyers. In recent years, there has been a significant increase in the number of litigants in person ("LIP"). This can be explained by a number of factors including the increasing cost of legal services and the greater availability of information from sources such as the Internet.

This book aims to provide practical advice on how to act for yourself and present a case in the civil courts of England and Wales, as well as presenting the basic principles of law and procedure. Information is given on some of the commonly encountered aspects of the law to ensure that a person acting for themself has a basic understanding of the legal issues so that they can make a reasoned decision as to whether they have a case to bring. However, legal advice should still be sought because in most cases a brief consultation with a legal professional is essential before embarking on any significant legal action.

Since the first edition came out in 2017, there have been some important events affecting court proceedings. The most notable being the severe impact of the COVID pandemic. The civil courts had to react quickly to keep the courts functioning and to facilitate this there was a greater use of remote online hearings. In the past, telephone hearings would usually only be used for short applications and where both parties were legallyl represented. Having come out of the COVID lockdowns, the use of remote hearings by Teams/Zoom and other forms of online platforms has continued. Being familiar and able to use online platforms is something which the Litigant in Person will now have to get to grips with. It has many advantages including reduced travel and less time hanging around court waiting rooms however there are obviously some disadvantages. It is not so easy to question a witness online and sometimes the technology does not work effectively.

This second edition also includes a new chapter explaining the different tracks which a defended claim can take depending on the size and nature of the claim. The claim might be allocated to the small claims track, fast track or multi track. Chapter 4 provides examples of how a case in each track is likely to proceed. In addition, there are new sections such as the guidance on what to do if you need to access your neighbour's land to undertake repairs to your property.

With court fees for civil claims having risen quite considerably in recent years, it is quite costly to start legal proceedings. Therefore, it is sensible to know beforehand if the case has merit and what procedures you should follow. Indeed, in some of the areas covered in this book it is made abundantly clear that you should seek legal advice and consider very carefully whether it would be appropriate to conduct such a claim without proper legal assistance. The absence of proper legal advice can lead to a litigant in person becoming a vexatious litigant. Vexatious litigants are people who persistently take legal action regardless of the merits of the claims. In serious cases, the court has powers to make an order which prevents the individual from making a legal claim without permission of the court.

This book refers to the litigant in person in the new legal world. The new legal world is a reference to various developments in the civil courts which began back in 1999 with the implementation of the Woolf reforms. Lord Woolf undertook a substantial reform of the procedural rules that apply to civil cases. The overriding objective of the Woolf reforms was to ensure that cases are dealt with justly and at proportionate cost. The Civil Procedure Rules

("CPR") were drafted in plain English to make them more understandable to those lay people using the courts. Since the Woolf reforms were implemented there have been many amendments and additions to the CPR so that the original aim of simplicity has been lost. There have been other changes to the civil procedural rules, such as the changes to the rules relating to costs introduced by Lord Jackson. These changes are moving towards a system of fixed costs so that a winning party is only able to recover a set amount from the losing party. This has probably also contributed to the increase in the number of litigants in person. If you are aware that even if you succeed in court action you will only be permitted to recover a fixed amount of costs from the loser, then you might be more likely to make a court claim without legal representation.

There has also been a stricter application of the sanctions that can be applied if a party fails to comply with court directions. One would have thought that a litigant in person would not have sanctions so rigidly applied against them compared to a party that has legal representation. However, legal cases have decided that litigants in person should not expect courts to be more lenient if they fail to carry out a step in a legal action by the required deadline.

Michael Langford
March 2023

Chapter 1

THE CIVIL COURTS AND LITIGATION

Ever since the introduction of the Woolf Reforms, there has been an emphasis in the court rules on "proportionality" when it comes to the amount of time spent on a case in relation to the cost and size of a claim and the importance/complexity of the issues involved. This principle can lead to small cases being considered as not worth taking to court. Deciding what is proportional in a particular case is not always easy and some lawyers have criticised the principle. That might be a matter of a vested interest protecting itself but sometimes making a decision as to what is proportional can be rather arbitrary; it is something you recognise when you see it but is rather hard to describe. It has also had an impact on the rise of the litigant in person ("LIP").

The increase in the LIP has also been influenced heavily by other factors, such as the removal of legal aid in virtually all areas of civil litigation. This book does not comment on the rights or wrongs of that decision but obviously if people on low incomes can no longer receive legal aid that will either mean they will represent themselves or not bring or defend a claim at all. It is more likely to mean that a party will act for themselves when defending a case than when bringing a claim. There is the possibility that a party may have legal expenses insurance but if a person is on a low or modest income they may decide not to have legal expenses insurance included in their policy. If you are on a modest income and searching for car or house insurance at the lowest possible price, you are likely to refuse legal expenses insurance in order to obtain the cheapest quote. It may seem that an extra £50 on the policy for legal expenses insurance may be good value for money, but if you are on a very tight budget then it is likely that you will want to trim as much off the price as possible and so legal expenses cover is often sacrificed.

Another factor in the rise of the LIP is the new approach to costs following on from the report of Lord Jackson. The introduction of costs budgets for multi-track cases (cases where damages claimed exceed £25,000) and the new approach to assessing costs, by making proportionality the key factor, led to the courts taking the view that the amount of the sums at stake is very important and the legal bills claimed by law firms should not generally be more than half of the damages awarded. The costs budgeting exercise has proved to take up too much court time, especially in cases at the lower end of the multi-track scale[1], and so there is soon to be the introduction of fixed recoverable legal fees. If litigants are not going to recover all or most of their costs, then they might consider doing more work themselves or perhaps instructing lawyers in a different way.

Lawyers may need to consider offering a variety of fee options as opposed to the traditional retainer where they act in all aspects of the case for an hourly rate, if they are going to attract certain clients in future. It may be that lawyers will have to offer so called "unbundled services" which means that they offer fixed fees for doing certain aspects of a case and are not necessarily on the court record. Some law firms, the Law Society and Insurers have concerns about unbundled services because they regard the arrangement as being riskier and having professional conduct issues. This nervousness about offering unbundled services may not make them widely available for a while. The nervousness arises from the fact that if a lawyer agrees to simply offer assistance in a particular aspect of a case but not to be recorded on the court file as acting in the claim, then there is a danger that

---

[1] Multi Track is usually for cases that are worth more than £25,000

the client may not be capable of handling or understanding the other aspects, or, the lawyer could be negligent in that they were not able to advise on a particular aspect as they did not have the whole picture before them. However, despite these worries expressed by lawyers, the Legal Services Board has encouraged lawyers to promote such services but, if you are a small to moderate sized firm, you would be wary of the client later suing you for negligence if things went wrong and you did not point out a particular risk. It may sound unlikely if the lawyer sets out the limitations of their work/advice but there have been cases where, notwithstanding this, the lawyer has been held responsible for not pointing out certain things. Lawyers are warier if clients come to them in cases where court action has already begun and they present themselves in the lawyer's office saying, "I have issued this claim/entered a defence to the case and now I need you to look at the witness statements I have drafted". Many lawyers will proceed with caution because it is not easy to pick up in the middle of matters especially where the LIP may have issued against the wrong individual or has defended the claim where there are no real grounds for defending. To be able to advise properly on a witness statement requires an understanding of all the facts of the case and sight of all the relevant documents. Sometimes clients who attend for advice in these types of situations do not always bring you all the "relevant documents" and will only bring along a selection of them. What may seem of little importance to the lay person is often of particular legal significance.

The Civil Courts Structure Review by Lord Justice Briggs was published in July 2016. His final report recommended an online court for claims up to the value of £25,000.

The report envisages the early stages of the process to a have a process which will filter a claim into a particular direction. Instead of a system whereby the Claimant enters his claim by completing a blank "Claim Form", the Claim Form will be produced online by answering a series of questions.

The County Court is currently operating an Online Civil Money Claims Pilot. Full details of of how and when it applies is contained in Practice Direction 51R. The extract below sets out the scope of this pilot:

SECTION 2 - SCOPE OF THE PILOT

2.1 Scope of this Pilot

2.1(1) The purpose of this practice direction is to establish a pilot to test an online claims process, called "Online Civil Money Claims". Claimants may use the pilot to make their claim, if their claim is suitable for the pilot. (Sub-paragraph (3) sets out the conditions that need to be met for a claim to be suitable for the pilot). The pilot is to run from 7th August 2017 to 30th November 2023. The pilot applies in the County Court.

2.1(2) Claims started using Online Civil Money Claims will be issued in the CTSC and will proceed there under the pilot unless they are sent out of the pilot. However, if this is not possible, the address for submitting documents in paper copy is: HMCTS CMC, PO Box 12747, Harlow, CM20 9RA.

2.1(3) Claim is only suitable for the pilot if all the following conditions are met–

(a) the claim is a claim for a specified amount of money only not exceeding the amount specified in paragraph 2.1(6) including interest;

(b) the claim would not ordinarily follow the Part 8 procedure;

(c) the claim is not being brought under the Consumer Credit Act 1974 unless it is brought under section 141 of that Act, to enforce a "regulated agreement" (as defined) relating only to money;

(d) either—

(i) the claimant will not be getting help with bringing the claim from a "legal representative" (as defined) and the claimant believes that the defendant will not be getting help with defending the claim from a "legal representative"; or

(ii) the claimant and the defendant are each represented by a legal representative, and the claimant will not, before submitting their claim, apply for remission or part remission of a fee prescribed by the Civil Proceedings Fees Order 2008;

It is sensible to make greater use of online technology especially in the area of producing trial bundles for hearings as there is a vast waste of paper as they do not get read. Using online technology can make the location of decision-making more flexible with parties and judges being able to participate without having to travel to a hearing centre. In cases that hinge on the interpretation of contracts and other documents, the benefits in terms of savings on the use of courts is obvious but there will always be cases where having the witnesses physically present is necessary. A judge could assess demeanour over a video link but that might not always be possible where you have a LIP without access to such technology or certain signals of credibility might not be conveyed so well over a video link. The report of Lord Briggs recommends that the traditional hearing where the parties turn up in person will not be the default position. Many have criticised this as it removes their "day in court" but as Lord Briggs confirms, many cases that cannot be settled will be directed to "face to face trial".

Summary

The civil court system to the objective observer is in a state of crisis. The county courts are underfunded and the government is considering ways to reduce the provision of judicial services and encouraging the use of alternative dispute resolution. The civil legal system is all about proportionality and complying with rules; the non-compliance with court rules is usually heavily sanctioned. In addition to centralising of the civil justice system, the government intends to set up online courts. One of the recent initiatives is that of an online court for claims up to £25,000.

❖❖❖

Chapter 2

HOW TO PREPARE A CASE

It is fundamental for anyone bringing a legal claim of any size or complexity to understand the basics of preparing and presenting the case in the most effective way. The first step is to lay out the facts as to what actually happened and then to consider the applicable law and apply it to the facts. This is a skill which lawyers are trained to perform. A lay person may not understand or be able to perform this task as competently as a lawyer although it is true from anecdotal evidence that there are many non-lawyers who are perfectly capable of making this assessment.

Even if the person is perfectly capable of constructing and assessing the case, a lawyer not only brings his legal training to the table but also their experience of how in practice the courts (and particular judges) will behave in certain situations. You could call this a certain "gut" feeling as to what in reality is going to happen in a particular situation. You could use the analogy of a graduate who has just achieved his degree and has the paper qualification to show he has passed various exams but does not have first-hand experience in the real world. In the legal world, experienced lawyers have a feel for how a court will exercise its discretion (if available to the judge). There are many examples that could be drawn on to illustrate this point. Knowing which way things are likely to go will save time and save paying out in legal costs for failed applications, which is important as court fees have increased.

Having a feel for when a court may make a particular decision is particularly relevant in certain applications in the county courts.

District Judges make decisions based on having heard the evidence and arguments from both sides and then applying the law to the facts to reach a decision with reasons for doing so. A lawyer will tell you that in reality there are a lot of factors which influence how a decision is made. Often, the factors explain why a judge does not actually make a decision and adjourns the matter. It is sometimes perceived (rightly or wrongly) that a Deputy District Judge in a county court might take the view that because he has a very busy list and a lack of time, they might be more inclined to adjourn a case (such as a claim for possession on non-mandatory grounds) rather than risk making a decision that might not stand up to scrutiny on appeal. It might for example be seen by the landlord as the court being too willing to exercise its discretion in favour of the tenant. Although this is particularly frustrating, as a LIP what you should take from this reality is that you must do everything in the preparation of your case to give yourself the best chance of the judge understanding very quickly what you are claiming or asking the court to decide.

To prepare a legal case, it is best to start with the basics and then put the meat on the bones. Equally, it should be noted that it is important to concentrate on the aspects of a claim that have a real chance of success and not to waste time on parts of a claim that are bound to fail. This point was made in a recent case of **Chambers v. Rooney (2017)** in which the court was considering an appeal against an earlier decision to strike out parts of a claim. The judgment has been described as an open letter from the High Court to litigants in person. Lord Justice Walker said:

...the course to be taken by litigants in person – and indeed by litigants who are represented – is to stand back and review the case. For litigants in person, a decision striking out parts of the claim will generally be a clear indication that they have been fighting on too many fronts, and that they need to stop wasting time and energy on parts of the claim that are bound to fail.
Those who conduct litigation in person need to appreciate that

steps which might redress any imbalance are more likely to assist if the litigant in person can stand back from the fray, and interpret what has been said by opponents and by the court objectively and in context.

To illustrate the process of breaking down the constituent elements of what you have to show to prove a claim, let us consider a contract claim.

CONTRACT CLAIM:

- Was there a contract?
- Was the contract written or oral?
- What were the terms of the contract?
- What term(s) of the contract has/have been breached?
- Has the breach been so fundamental that it allows you to end the contract?
- What loss have you suffered directly as a result of the breach of contract?

These are the fundamental questions you should ask yourself when considering a claim for a breach of contract. Each of these elements will fit together to establish your claim (or not as the case may be). You will need to present evidence (either in documentary form or by way of oral evidence) to establish these aspects and if the judge is satisfied on the balance of probability, then you should win your case.

It is useful to take each of these elements of a contract claim in turn.

Was there a contract?

This is the starting point, which may sound obvious in a contract claim but many LIPs do not give it sufficient thought. It does not mean was there simply something in writing, as contracts can be in writing or verbal (except in certain cases) but were the key ingredients present to make it an Agreement that is enforceable. In simple terms, without getting into technical legal arguments, a contract is:

When one person makes an offer, and another person accepts it by communicating their assent or performing the offer's terms.

English law also requires that before an agreement can be enforced there must be what is known as "consideration". It must show that they have brought something to the bargain which has "something of value in the eyes of the law". A simple example of consideration is where an offer to purchase a car for £5,000 is made and accepted. The consideration is the £5,000. When a contract is formed, good consideration is needed and so a mere promise is not binding. If Mr Bloggs says to Mr Jones, "I promise to pay you £5,000", then that is simply an unenforceable promise as there is no consideration. If Mr Bloggs breaks his promise to pay the £5,000 then Mr Jones would not be able to sue Mr Bloggs. There are some cases where promises are enforceable without consideration but there are certain requirements such as the fact that the agreement must be signed as a deed.

In many situations, the consideration is easily identifiable but there will be a few situations where, although it looks on the surface as consideration is present, it may not meet the principles of contract law such as where it is "past consideration". This is getting into territory that is too technical for a what a LIP needs to know and if such an argument arises then that would be the point to obtain legal advice.

Was the contract written or oral?

Contrary to common belief, contracts which are oral can be enforceable unless there is something in law which requires them to be evidenced in writing. An example of when a contract must be in writing to be enforceable is that of a contract to sell land. An estate agent's sale board will say "sold subject to contract" because although the seller of the house may have said to a buyer, "I agree to sell my house to you. for £X", until it is put into a written contract signed by both parties there is not a binding agreement. (The position is different under Scottish law where the acceptance of an offer to purchase is binding.)

Although oral contracts are enforceable, if the contract is for something important it is obvious to see that if a dispute arises then there might be a problem proving the terms of the agreement. It is still surprising how often businesses will conduct trade in important areas without putting anything of the agreement in writing. It may not always be necessary to have a formally written document signed by both parties but it is certainly advisable to at least confirm the verbally agreed terms in correspondence soon after an agreement is made.

What were the terms of the contract?

An agreement will generally consist of various terms. Even the simplest of contracts will have terms. The main terms generally being the price paid and the subject matter of the contract, e.g. the goods or services provided. It is usual for businesses to have standard written terms which can be quite lengthy. There are "express" and "implied terms" in a contract. An express term is stated by the parties during negotiation or written in a contractual document. Implied terms are not stated but nevertheless form a provision of the contract. An implied term may, for example, be in a contract because of a statutory provision or it may be implied through other ways such as by business efficacy or the fact that the implied terms are so obvious that it goes without saying.

What terms of the contract have been breached?

It is important to understand the nature of a particular term in a contract. Some terms (called conditions) are so important and go to the root of the contract. If a condition is breached, then the innocent party is entitled to regard the contract as at an end and can claim damages. Less important terms may not allow an innocent party to regard the contract as at an end but may be able to claim damages. Payment is going to be an important term of a contract. If the innocent party has not received payment, then they would usually be entitled to end the contract and claim the unpaid amount that is due.

What loss have you suffered directly because of the breach of contract?

Damages in contract law are a legal remedy available for breach of contract. Damages are an award of money to compensate the innocent party. The primary purpose of damages in contract law is to place the injured party in the position they would have been in had the contract been performed. An award of damages in contract law is subject to the application of the rules on causation, remoteness and a duty to mitigate loss. Under the rules of remoteness of damage in contract law, a claimant may only recover losses which may reasonably be considered as arising naturally from the breach or such damages which may reasonably be in the contemplation of the parties at the time the contract was made. This principle, as to what amount of damages can be recovered, is illustrated by the case of:

Hadley v. Baxendale [1854]:

In this case, the crankshaft broke in the Claimant's mill. He engaged the services of the Defendant to deliver the crankshaft to the place where it was to be repaired and to subsequently return it after it had been repaired. Due to neglect of the Defendant, the crankshaft was returned 7 days late. The Claimant was unable to use the mill during this time and claimed for loss of profit. The Defendant argued that he was unaware that the mill would have to be closed during the delay and therefore the loss of profit was too remote. It was held that the damages available for breach of contract include:

1. Those which may fairly and reasonably be considered arisingnaturally from the breach of contract **or**
2. Such damages as may reasonably be supposed to have been in the contemplation of both the parties at the time the contract was made.

The court declined to allow Hadley to recover lost profits in this case, holding that Baxendale could only be held liable for losses that were generally foreseeable, or if Hadley had mentioned his special circumstances in advance.

Negligence claim:

The same exercise can be used with other potential claims you may be thinking of bringing. If you think that your claim is one of negligence then you break it down in to the constituent parts of such a claim. There are there three basic elements to establishing a negligence claim:

1. Did the defendant owe you a duty of care?
2. What is the standard of care and did the defendant breach that duty of care?
3. Did the breach of that duty cause the loss/damage?

Do you have the evidence to prove your claim?

It may seem obvious, but having sufficient evidence to convince the judge on the balance of probability that you have proved your case is the key to any civil legal action. Litigants in person, especially those who see their case more as a crusade rather than as an unfortunate dispute that needs resolving, can become so convinced that they are right and that everybody else is wrong that they forget the key ingredient of relevant evidence. When you act for yourself it is difficult to stand back and be objective as to whether you have a real prospect of success. What a litigant in person should do is to sit down with a piece of paper and lay out what needs to be proved and what evidence they have (or are likely to have) to satisfy that part of the claim. So, for example, suppose you have employed a builder to build an extension at your property and you are not happy with the end result. You are going to need some form of independent evidence (most likely from a building surveyor) to comment on the nature of the defects and what was the cause of them. If you have suffered loss as a result of the defects, then you will need evidence to support the costs involved in rectifying the defects.

Summary:

To the ordinary person, when you believe you have been wronged or something is unfair, it is easy to jump to the conclusion that you have a cause of action. Breaking down your claim into its individual elements will demonstrate whether you can show a cause of action. It may be that there has been a breach of contract, for example, but you are not going to be able to bring a claim if you cannot show that you have suffered a loss as a result of the breach. Or it might be that a person/professional that owed you a duty of care might breach the duty they owe you when you consider the standard of care expected of them. Breaking down your potential claim into its constituent parts when preparing a case will also enable you to see at an early stage whether you will require further evidence to prove a particular point.

❖❖❖

Chapter 3

THE STAGES OF LITIGATION

Having determined whether your proposed claim has legal merit, there will then be several steps in the civil court rules which you have to go through before you get anywhere near a decision at trial. The ordinary person finds this frustrating. When someone throws down the challenge of "I'll see you in court", it is often said with the effect of being an announcement of what is just around the corner if the other person does not give in to your demands. Anybody with a slight knowledge of the civil justice system will know that in most cases this is very far from reality. Going to court is not like making an appointment to see your doctor. You don't just ring up the court and ask for an appointment in the next week or so. For several reasons, there have been layers of procedure introduced which you must go through before you can expect to have your day in court.

Pre-action Protocols and letters of claim

As a litigant in person, the first stage of the long legal journey is to send correspondence to the other party which is compliant with the pre-action protocol. The civil procedure rules contain several pre-action protocols for certain areas of law. Where there is not a specific protocol, there is a practice direction outlining the principles that must be complied with before commencing court action. At present, there are the following pre-action protocols:

Protocol	Came into force
Personal Injury	6 April 2015
Resolution of Clinical Disputes	6 April 2015
Construction and Engineering (2nd edition)	17 February 2017
Defamation	2 October 2000
Professional Negligence	16 July 200
Judicial Review	6 April 2015
Disease and Illness	8 December 2008
Housing Disrepair	6 April 2015
Possession Claims by Social Landlords	6 April 2015
Possession Claims for Mortgage Arrears	6 April 2015
Dilapidation of Commercial Property	1 January 2012
Low Value Personal Injury Road Traffic Accident Claims	30 April 2010 (extended from 31 July 2013)
Low Value Personal Injury Employers' and Public Liability Claims	31 July 2013
Debt Claims	1 October 2017

All of the above Pre-Action Protocols (along with all of the Civil Procedure Rules) can be viewed on the Ministry of Justice web site: https://www.justice.gov.uk/courts/procedure-rules/civil

If none of the above specific protocols apply, then regard should be given to the Practice Directions which state:

PRACTICE DIRECTION – PRE-ACTION CONDUCT AND PROTOCOLS
Introduction

1 *Pre-action protocols explain the conduct and set out the steps the court would normally expect parties to take before commencing proceedings for particular types of civil claims. They are approved by the Master of the Rolls and are annexed to the Civil Procedure Rules (CPR). (The current pre-action protocols are listed in paragraph 18.)*

2. This Practice Direction applies to disputes where no pre-action protocol approved by the Master of the Rolls applies.

Objectives of pre-action conduct and protocols

3. Before commencing proceedings, the court will expect the parties to have exchanged sufficient information to—

(a) understand each other's position;
(b) make decisions about how to proceed;
(c) try to settle the issues without proceedings;
(d) consider a form of Alternative Dispute Resolution (ADR) to assist with settlement;
(e) support the efficient management of those proceedings; and
(f) reduce the costs of resolving the dispute.

Proportionality

4. A pre-action protocol or this Practice Direction must not be used by a party as a tactical device to secure an unfair advantage over another party. Only reasonable and proportionate steps should be taken by the parties to identify, narrow and resolve the legal, factual or expert issues.

5. The costs incurred in complying with a pre-action protocol or this Practice Direction should be proportionate (CPR 44.3(5)). Where parties incur disproportionate costs in complying with any pre-action protocol or this Practice Direction, those costs will not be recoverable as part of the costs of the proceedings.

Steps before issuing a claim at court

6. Where there is a relevant pre-action protocol, the parties should comply with that protocol before commencing proceedings. Where there is no relevant pre-action protocol, the parties should exchange correspondence and information to comply with the objectives in paragraph 3, bearing in mind that compliance should be proportionate. The steps will usually include—

(a) the claimant writing to the defendant with concise details of the claim. The letter should include the basis on which the claim is made, a summary of the facts, what the claimant wants from the defendant, and if money, how the amount is calculated;

(b) *the defendant responding within a reasonable time - 14 days in a straight forward case and no more than 3 months in a very complex one. The reply should include confirmation as to whether the claim is accepted and, if it is not accepted, the reasons why, together with an explanation as to which facts and parts of the claim are disputed and whether the defendant is making a counterclaim as well as providing details of any counterclaim; and*

(c) *the parties disclosing key documents relevant to the issues in dispute.*

Experts

7. *Parties should be aware that the court must give permission before expert evidence can be relied upon (see CPR 35.4(1)) and that the court may limit the fees recoverable. Many disputes can be resolved without expert advice or evidence. If it is necessary to obtain expert evidence, particularly in low value claims, the parties should consider using a single expert, jointly instructed by the parties, with the costs shared equally.*

Settlement and ADR

8. *Litigation should be a last resort. As part of a relevant pre-action protocol or this Practice Direction, the parties should consider whether negotiation or some other form of ADR might enable them to settle their dispute without commencing proceedings.*

9. *Parties should continue to consider the possibility of reaching a settlement at all times, including after proceedings have been started. Part 36 offers may be made before proceedings are issued.*

10. *Parties may negotiate to settle a dispute or may use a form of ADR including—*

(a) *mediation, a third party facilitating a resolution;*

(b) *arbitration, a third party deciding the dispute;*

(c) *early neutral evaluation, a third party giving an informed opinion on the dispute; and*

(d) *Ombudsmen schemes.*

(Information on mediation and other forms of ADR is available in the Jackson ADR Handbook (available from Oxford University Press)

11. *If proceedings are issued, the parties may be required by the court to provide evidence that ADR has been considered. A party's silence in response to an invitation to participate or a refusal to participate in ADR might be considered unreasonable by the court and could lead to the court ordering that party to pay additional court costs.*

Stocktake and list of issues

12. *Where a dispute has not been resolved after the parties have followed a pre-action protocol or this Practice Direction, they should review their respective positions. They should consider the papers and the evidence to see if proceedings can be avoided and at least seek to narrow the issues in dispute before the claimant issues proceedings.*

Compliance with this Practice Direction and the Protocols

13. *If a dispute proceeds to litigation, the court will expect the parties to have complied with a relevant pre-action protocol or this Practice Direction. The court will take into account non-compliance when giving directions for the management of proceedings (see CPR 3.1(4) to (6)) and when making orders for costs (see CPR 44.3(5)(a)). The court will consider whether all parties have complied in substance with the terms of the relevant pre-action protocol or this Practice Direction and is not likely to be concerned with minor or technical infringements, especially when the matter is urgent (for example an application for an injunction).*

14. *The court may decide that there has been a failure of compliance when a party has—*

(a) not provided sufficient information to enable the objectives in paragraph 3 to be met;

(b) not acted within a time limit set out in a relevant protocol, or within a reasonable period; or

(c) unreasonably refused to use a form of ADR, or failed to respond at all to an invitation to do so.

15. *Where there has been non-compliance with a pre-action protocol or this Practice Direction, the court may order that*

(a) the parties are relieved of the obligation to comply or further comply with the pre-action protocol or this Practice Direction;

(b) the proceedings are stayed while particular steps are taken to comply with the pre-action protocol or this Practice Direction;

(c) sanctions are to be applied.

16. The court will consider the effect of any non-compliance when deciding whether to impose any sanctions which may include—

(a) an order that the party at fault pays the costs of the proceedings, or part of the costs of the other party or parties;

(b) an order that the party at fault pay those costs on an indemnity basis;

(c) if the party at fault is a claimant who has been awarded a sum of money, an order depriving that party of interest on that sum for a specified period, and/or awarding interest at a lower rate than would otherwise have been awarded;

(d) if the party at fault is a defendant, and the claimant has been awarded a sum of money, an order awarding interest on that sum for a specified period at a higher rate, (not exceeding 10% above base rate), than the rate which would otherwise have been awarded.

Limitation

17. This Practice Direction and the pre-action protocols do not alter the statutory time limits for starting court proceedings. If a claim is issued after the relevant limitation period has expired, the defendant will be entitled to use that as a defence to the claim. If proceedings are started to comply with the statutory time limit before the parties have followed the procedures in this Practice Direction or the relevant pre-action protocol, the parties should apply to the court for a stay of the proceedings while they so comply.

The litigant in person may ask the question, why the need for pre-action protocols? The idea of pre-action protocols emerged from the Woolf Reforms of 1999 so that parties to a dispute would have to set out their case and exchange more information before starting the legal process. By doing this, each side has a better understanding of the other's case and this provides a better opportunity to settle a case without court action commencing.

With the early disclosure of documents, a party may discover at that point that their case has little prospect of succeeding and so take a realistic view to either drop the claim or reach a sensible compromise. This objective has a sound basis but what has happened with passage of time since Woolf, is that the pre-action protocols have expanded and have added a considerable burden in terms of extra legal costs (where you have legal representation) and additional time into the legal process.

Although the Rules make clear that the pre-action protocols are not expected to be used as a tactical device, the reality is that they are and so those who do not following them will face cries from the other side that they will apply to stay proceedings if they start action before the protocol has been fully complied with. This threat has become quite popular but, with the increase in court fees for making an application, the chances are that if you start a claim without following the whole of the pre-action process the likelihood of the defendant making such an application is slight. More likely that the Defendant will simply ask for extra time to prepare the Defence. Failure to comply with pre-action protocols is a factor when costs come to be decided, but as not many cases will go all the way to a contested trial, the worry that your haste in starting legal action might be punished by cost sanctions may not necessarily be a real concern.

The key thing with pre-action protocol is to try and comply with the spirit of a protocol if not necessarily the letter of each protocol. I say this because it is likely that the average person is probably not going to be involved in bringing a claim in an area that involves a protocol apart from perhaps housing disrepair and construction and engineering. These two protocols would cover a situation of a tenant making a claim against a landlord for the property being in a state of disrepair or an action involving substandard work by a building contractor.

The protocol that a litigant in person is most likely to encounter is the general one where no specific protocol exists. The requirements of this, as a can be seen from the Practice Direction set out in full above, are not particularly onerous. It is perfectly reasonable for the claimant to be expected to set out in writing, *"concise details of the claim"*. The letter should, *"include the basis on which the claim is made, a summary of the facts, what the claimant wants from the defendant, and if money, how the amount is calculated."* The expected response from the Defendant is equally reasonable:

> b) *the defendant responding within a reasonable time - 14 days in a straight forward case and no more than 3 months in a very complex one. The reply should include confirmation as to whether the claim is accepted and, if it is not accepted, the reasons why, together with an explanation as to which facts and parts of the claim are disputed and whether the defendant is making a counterclaim as well as providing details of any counterclaim; and*

> (c) *the parties disclosing key documents relevant to the issues in dispute.*

Alternative Dispute Resolution (ADR)

Where the protocol goes wrong, in my view, is the placing of too much the emphasis on considering alternative ways to achieve *"settlement"*. Whilst one should not rush to court, the use of the phrase settlement always seems to be aimed at a compromise. Why not use the word "decision" instead? One suspects that those in charge of the Civil Justice system want to put obstacles in the way of a having a day in court to save money and therefore they place emphasis on settlement. Professor Genn famously said in the Hamlyn Lectures of 2008 that, *"Mediation is not about just settlement. It is just about settlement."* She rightly summed up the objective in recent years of downgrading the Civil Justice system and pushing parties into mediation. Perhaps the emphasis of alternative dispute resolution has wrongly spent too much time promoting mediation, whereas what the court user wants is a binding decision to be made as cheaply and efficiently as possible. Mediations by their very nature do not decide an issue but try and facilitate a settlement to be reached. The reality is that we all know it means persuading the parties to reach a compromise by frightening each side by the risk of massive legal costs if they do not settle and proceed to trial. Whilst it is right that a litigant should be warned of the realities of failing, is it right that a party should be frightened by fear of the unknown into agreeing a settlement at a mediation? The point I make is that litigants in person should consider the alternatives to court action but should perhaps be aware that mediation is not the only alternative way of bringing a dispute to an end.

Arbitration

With the recent high increases in court fees for claims over £10,000, there is a strong argument for cost controlled arbitration along the lines of the schemes on offer from the Chartered Institute of Arbitrators (CIArb). The Business Arbitration Scheme (BAS) aims to provide a simple and cost-effective form of arbitration for claims over £5,000 to £100,000 in value. To commence the BAS process, each party must pay a fixed fee of £1,250 plus VAT which covers administrative costs and the fees of the arbitrator. An arbitrator is then appointed by the chairperson of the applicant's local branch of the CIArb within ten days of commencement of the arbitration. The process results in a legally binding outcome to the dispute in less than 90 days from the appointment of the arbitrator. One of the key attractions to users is the limit of £1,000 on legal fees which are recoverable by the winner from the other party to the dispute. A party can incur greater costs if it so desires, but it will not be able to recover them from the losing party. The process has been designed without the need for extensive legal representation if indeed any legal representation at all.

Mediation

The question which should be posed about mediation is why would you spend a sum of money in the hope of arriving at a settlement as opposed to spending the same sum of money for a decision to be made one way or the other at arbitration? Although it seems logical to go for the certainty of having a decision, there will be occasions when mediation has its attractions. It is a case of being able to spot the situation when mediation is appropriate. It will probably be an occasion where you want to maintain control over the outcome and this is probably where it is difficult to assess the outcome of the evidence. In such circumstances, mediation can have the benefit of testing the theories and strengths of your case and this probing could lead to an acceptable solution. If you have a dispute which is finely balanced, and both parties appear receptive to communication from the other, then the chance of reaching a settlement is quite likely. Experience makes you recognise these situations.

To illustrate the style and content of pre-action compliant letters of claim, let us consider the following example:

Fred Watts v. John Frindell
Fred Watts bought a sports car from Mr Frindell, a dealer, for £15,000. Two months later, Mr Watts was stopped by the Police and the car was impounded as it had been stolen. It was then returned to the rightful owner. Mr Watts decided to bring a claim against Mr Frindell.

The basis of the claim by Fred Watts against Mr Frindell is that there is an implied term that a seller of goods must have legal title to sell the goods.

Dear Mr. Frindell,

LETTER OF CLAIM
This is my letter of claim sent in accordance with the Practice Direction Pre-Action Conduct and Protocols of the Civil Procedure Rules 1998. I draw your attention to the final section of this letter, which sets out the deadline by which your response is required, and the consequences of failing to respond properly within that time.

1   Basis of claim
1.1   *I purchased a Mazda Sports Car (the 'Car') from you for the sum of £15,000 on xx/xx/xx. Ten days after purchasing the car, I was stopped by the Police who informed me that the Car had previously been stolen. They seized the Car and returned it to its true owner. Therefore, there has been a total failure of consideration in that I received nothing for the money I paid to you and so therefore seek the return of that amount.*

1.2   *There was an implied term in the contract by the Consumer Consumer Rights Act 2015 that you had the right to sell the Car to me or that you would have such a right at the time when title to the Car was to pass. As the Car was returned to its true owner, the consideration of £15,000 that I paid for the Car has totally failed.*

1.3   *Accordingly, I intend to pursue a claim against you for the recovery of the sum of £15,000 because the consideration that I paid has totally failed, I received nothing in return for the money.*

2   Next steps
2.1   *As noted above, this letter of claim has been prepared and sent to you in accordance with the Practice Direction on Pre-Action Conduct and Protocols. In accordance with the Pre-Action protocols, I expect a response to this letter within a reasonable time. A period of 14 days is a reasonable time in the circumstances of this case. Accordingly, I require your response to this letter by* [insert deadline, including an additional two days to

allow for service]. *Your reply should include confirmation as to whether the claim is accepted and, if it is not accepted, the reasons why, together with an explanation as to which facts are disputed.*

2.2   *If you ignore this letter it will lead to me starting proceedings which will increase your liability for costs.*

Yours faithfully

Fred Watts

Commencing Court Action

A court action is commenced by completing a Claim Form and sending it to the court office along with the fee. However, you cannot now start a money claim by popping down to your local county court. The majority of claims, including money claims, are started by using the procedure contained in Part 7 of the Civil Procedure Rules and are therefore referred to as "Part 7 Claims".

There are a number of ways to start a claim for money:

1. By sending paper copies to County Court Money Claims Centre.

At the time of writing this second edition, the County Court Money Claims Centre (CCMC) is located in Salford, Greater Manchester. It has been decided that the CCMC will be merged with the County Business Centre in Northampton and eventually the building in Salford will no longer be used.

2. Issuing a claim using Money Claim Online

Issuing a claim via Money Claim Online (MCOL). The website address for MCOL is:
https://www.moneyclaim.gov.uk/web/mcol/welcome

Claims issued in MCOL must be:

- for a fixed amount of money less than £100,000
- for no more than one claimant and against no more than 2 defendants (people or organisations)
- served to a defendant or defendant(s) with an address in England or Wales

To make a claim in MCOL you need:

- a valid credit or debit card to pay the court fees
- an address in the United Kingdom
- an email address
- regular access to a computer and the internet

You cannot use MCOL if you are:

- under 18 years old
- eligible for legal aid, or eligible for 'Help with fees'
- making a claim for compensation for an accident or injury
- prevented by the court from making claims because you are a 'vexatious litigant' (someone who uses court cases to harass other people)
- intending to issue a joint Warrant of Control
- issuing any new claim, entering judgment by default or requesting a warrant against a defendant or anyone who is jointly liable with them whilst any of them are in a breathing space scheme

You cannot use MCOL to make a claim against:

- a child under 18
- someone who lacks 'mental capacity' (someone unable to make their own decisions)
- a government department or agency, for example HMRC or DVLA
- an individual or company as a result of a tribunal award
- claims relating to the Tenancy Deposit Scheme should not be issued in MCOL

3. Online Civil Money Claims Pilot.

This new pilot service can be accessed on the Government website at the following address:
https://www.moneyclaims.service.gov.uk/eligibility#

Claims which are not Part 7 Claims, can be started in your local county court. Civil Procedure Rule Part 8 governs many of these claims. The Part 8 procedure is usually for claims such as injunctions and declarations, e.g. asking the court to interpret a lease. These claims usually do not involve major disputes of fact. In the case of interpreting a lease, there is unlikely to be a dispute of fact and simply a matter for the court to decide the meaning of certain clauses in the lease. The rules also state that certain types of claim must be started by using the Part 8 procedure, such as claims for harassment under the Protection from Harassment Act 1997, claims for the return of goods or claims under the Inheritance (Provision for Family & Dependants) Act 1975. An example of an inheritance claim is contained in Chapter 8.

Claims for the possession of land can be started in your local county court. Such claims involving residential property can also be conducted online by using PCOL (Possession Claim Online). Again, if you issue possession proceedings online there is a saving in respect of the court fee to commence the action. The procedure to follow for claiming possession of property is contained in Civil Procedure Rules Part 55. Possession Claims.

A typical Part 7 claim is a claim for money due to a breach of contract or a simple debt action. The Claim is started by completing a Claim Form (form N1). A Part 8 Claim is started by completing a different type of Claim Form, form N208. The procedure in respect of Part 8 claims is different compared to Part 7 claims in that when you start a Part 8 claim you need to file your written evidence when you issue the claim, whereas in a Part 7 claim, the claim form sets out sufficient information about the nature of the claim so that the defendant knows the claim being brought against them.

If the claim is defended, then there are stages in the process (known as "directions") which require the parties to do certain things in order to prepare the case for trial.

In a Part 7 claim, the stages are usually as follows:

1. Issue the claim and serve it on the Defendant
2. The Defendant files a defence within the required time
3. If defended, complete a Directions Questionnaire
4. Directions given or a case management hearing
5. The directions usually include:

   - Disclosure
   - Witness statements
   - Expert evidence if permitted by the court
   - Completion of Listing Questionnaires
   - Pre-Trial Review hearing
   - The Trial Date plus length and location of trial

With Part 8 claims after the Claim is issued, the Defendant does not have to file a formal defence but instead when they file the Acknowledgement of Service within 14 days, the Defendant must file and serve their written evidence. The Defendant can ask the Claimant for an extension of 14 days to file and serve their evidence in a part 8, but, for a longer extension, an application to the court is required. If a Defendant in a Part 8 claim does not file an acknowledgement of service, then the Defendant is not able to take any further part in the proceedings. A Claimant though is not able to obtain judgment in default in a Part 8 claim. Once the acknowledgement of service has been filed by the Defendant, the court will usually set a date for a disposal or directions hearing. It is quite possible that where the issue in dispute is relatively straightforward and not too complicated, the judge will decide the case at the disposal hearing; this would probably be the case, for example, if the court is asked to decide a concise issue, such as deciding what property is included in a lease, which would only require the judge to interpret the wording of the Lease.

Court Directions after a claim is defended (Part 7 claims)

Having issued court proceedings, you do not suddenly end up with a trial date a few weeks later. This impression might be created from watching television dramas. However, the litigant in person needs to be aware that for claims outside the small claims track [claims above £10,000 and complicated cases involving difficult points of law] there are many stages to go through before you reach the trial. Litigants in person should not think that because they are not represented the court will take a lenient approach to the compliance with court directions. Case law has made it clear that the new strict approach to complying with deadlines applies in the same way to litigants in person as it does to those with legal representation. It is a whole lot more difficult for vexatious litigants to play the system and delay a trial.

Court Directions and case management

If a claim is defended then the court will send out Directions Questionnaires to each party to complete and return to court. There is a brief version of the Directions Questionnaire in small claims but for fast track and multi-track cases the Directions Questionnaire is longer and requires more information. From looking at the Statement of Case (Claim Form and Defence) and the Directions Questionnaire, the District Judge will allocate the case to the appropriate track. If the claim is allocated to the fast track (claims above £10,000 but not exceeding £25,000) the judge will give a list of fairly standard and straightforward directions which the parties must follow and comply with to prepare the case ready for trial. A fast track matter will probably not have a case management conference and the trial will usually have a "trial window" about 6 months after it has been allocated. Typical directions for the fast track might be:

1. By [the date] both parties are to undertake standard disclosure by way of serving a list of documents in form N265.
2. By [date] the parties are to provide inspection of any document on their list within 7 days of a request for inspection by providing copies of the document.
3. By [date] the parties are to serve signed statements of all oral evidence to be given at trial by witnesses.

In a case that may require expert evidence, a party seeking to use the evidence of an expert at trial must seek a direction from the court for permission to do so. Therefore, in cases where expert evidence is relevant, the judge will give a direction stating that there is permission to use expert evidence and whether the expert will be a single and jointly instructed expert, or whether each party is permitted to instruct their own expert.

Disclosure

In many cases, especially those which are not particularly complicated and do not involve significant amounts of documents and or documents stored electronically, the direction as to disclosure is likely to be that of 'standard disclosure'. The court rules state that under standard disclosure, a party must disclose to the other side the following:

- Documents on which he relies
- documents which adversely affect his own case
- documents which adversely affect another party's case or support another party's case, and
- the documents he is required to disclose by any relevant practice direction

A document is defined in the court rules as anything on which information of any description is recorded. Thus, a document is not confined to paper but includes electronic documents, audio and video cassettes, as well as other similar material. Electronic documents include emails, messages on mobile phones, word processed documents and databases. A party must disclose documents which are now, or have been previously within their control. The meaning of control is where a party has a document or had the document in their physical possession, has or had a right to possession of the document, or the party has or had a right to inspect or take copies of it. A party in litigation must undertake a reasonable search for documents. The extent of the search must be proportionate. It should be remembered that without prejudice correspondence should not be disclosed. If a document has been headed 'without prejudice save as to costs' then that document can only be relied upon after the trial when issues of cost come to be decided.

Disclosure takes place in two stages. First, each party must complete a list of documents in its control and then once the list of documents has been exchanged, a party may inspect any documents they don't have, usually by requesting the other party to provide copies.

The list of documents is completed on the court form N265. A copy of this document is shown at the end of this chapter. As can be seen, the form is broken down into three parts. These are documents which the party does not object to being inspected, documents presently in the party's control to which there is an objection to inspection and documents which have been but are no longer in their control. A party will have to give a reason why they object to the disclosure of certain documents and usually it is because these documents are privileged such as legal professional privilege. Those documents with legal professional privilege relate to correspondence between a party and their solicitor who is giving advice in relation to the proceedings. This will also include opinions the party has obtained from counsel. Form N265 must have the declaration on it signed by the party and not their legal representative. The disclosure statement confirms that the party signing it believes the extent of the search to have been reasonable in all the circumstances. The fact that the disclosure statement on form N265 must be signed by the party, is sometimes overlooked by solicitors. However, it is important and, until the disclosure statement has been signed by the party, disclosure has not been completed.

Once you receive the list of documents from the other side, you should request any copies you require within the time scale stated on the court directions, usually within seven days of receiving the list of documents. Upon receiving the other parties documents it is important to quickly examine what you have received and decide on whether you accept the authenticity of those documents. The authenticity of documents disclosed is deemed to be admitted unless a party serves a notice in form N268 requiring that party to prove at trial. A notice to prove a document must be served by the latest date for serving witness statements or within seven days of disclosure of that document whichever is the later. In cases where a document is disputed, for example where a party produces copies of diary entries that have been handwritten and you think those handwritten entries have been added later, then serving a notice to prove the document would be of benefit as that would require the party disclosing the document to give evidence or produce the originals at trial.

It should be remembered that you have a continuing duty to disclose until the end of proceedings. What this means is that if documents come into your possession after serving your list of documents, then these new documents must be disclosed to the other side.

It should be remembered that the rules relating to disclosure do not apply to cases allocated to the small claims track, namely cases which do not exceed £10,000 in value. There is provision within part 27 of the civil procedure rules for a judge to order a party to give further information in a small claims track. However, the lack of rules in relation to disclosure in small claims track cases, means that if you think the other party is withholding an important document, then you must consider making an application for either pre-action disclosure or specific disclosure before the case is allocated to the small claims track. Otherwise, once the case is allocated to the small claims track, it may well be difficult to get the other party to show that document at the small claims hearing because there is no duty for a party to disclose a document in a small claim. The reason why the rules relating to small claims track cases are less detailed and exclude provisions relating to disclosure, is that small claims hearings are intended to be less formal and hopefully a more swift method for disposing of cases. However, small claims do, as this matter relating to disclosure illustrates, have their limitations and suffer criticism from some for being a rather rough and ready approach to justice. Cases up to £10,000 are regarded in legal terms as being 'small' but to many ordinary people and also small businesses, claims up to £10,000 are not necessarily that small as a sum of just below £10,000 could be deemed a significant amount of money to them.

The disclosure outlined above is that of standard disclosure and what should be remembered is that when you complete the directions questionnaire for a multi-track claim (usually cases which exceed £25,000 in value) then there is a further stage in the process to complete a directions report where both parties comment on the broad range of documents that are in the possession of the parties and to suggest which type of disclosure would be appropriate. It might be that the parties agree to a proposal that disclosure should be dispensed with, or there be standard disclosure or some other appropriate direction as to disclosure which meets the overriding objective in the court rules. If the type disclosure can't be agreed then the court will give a direction.

At the end of this chapter, is a sample List of Documents to show how the form N265 should be completed.

Witness statements

The court will normally give a direction that witness statements should be exchanged prior to the trial. This is likely to be the case even in small claims hearings. A witness statement is a written statement signed by a person which contains the evidence which that person would be allowed to give orally. The contents of the statement must as far as possible be in the witness's own words and should be expressed in the first person. The two main purposes of a witness statement is to provide evidence in support of interim applications, but mainly the setting out of the evidence which witnesses are permitted to give at trial. What is often forgotten by litigants in person is that a witness statement should not be used as a vehicle for conveying legal argument. It should also not give opinions (although there are a few limited exceptions) and should merely set out what the witness had direct experience of, i.e. what they saw or heard. A sample witness statement is at the end of this chapter.

A witness statement should not contain submissions or convey legal argument:

This is a very common problem with witness statement s drafted by lawyers let alone litigants in person. There have been many cases where the courts have been very critical of witness statements which seem to go on forever and to contain large quotations from case law. It should be remembered what the court rules say on what a witness statement is:

> CPR Part 32.4(1)
> *"A witness statement is a written statement signed by a person which contains the evidence which that person would be allowed to give orally."*

You cannot give evidence of what the law is.

There are a number of cases which provide clear examples of where a witness statement oversteps the mark. In particular the case of *JD Wetherspoon PLC v. Jason Harris* **[2013] EWHC 1088 (Ch)** is a very good illustration of a witness statement which crossed the line into making submissions The case concerned alleged dishonest dealings in relation to property transactions. The claimant made an application for summary judgment and also that parts of the evidence of a witness, Mr Goldberger, be struck out. The summary judgment application was not successful. However, the application to strike out the evidence was successful. Mr Goldberger had not been involved with the defendant company at the time of the transaction and so could not give direct evidence. The judge observed that:

> *"The vast majority of Mr Goldberger's witness statement contains a recitation of facts based on the documents, commentary on those documents, argument, submissions and expressions of opinion, particularly on aspects of the commercial property market."*

In his judgment, Sir Terence Etherton looked at the rules relating to witness statements:

> *"38. CPR r.32.4 describes a witness statement as: 'a written statement signed by a person which contains the evidence which that person would be allowed to give orally'.*
>
> *39. Mr Goldberger would not be allowed at trial to give oral evidence which merely recites the relevant events, of which he does not have direct knowledge, by reference to documents he has read. Nor would he be permitted at trial to advance arguments and make submissions which might be expected of an advocate rather than a witness of fact. These points are made clear in paragraph 7 of Appendix 9 to the Chancery Guide (7th ed), which is as follows:*
>
> *A witness statement should simply cover those issues, but only those issues, on which the party serving the statement wishes that witness to give evidence in chief. Thus it is not, for example, the function of a*

witness statement to provide a commentary on the documents in the trial bundle, nor to set out quotations from such documents, nor to engage in matters of argument. Witness statements should not deal with other matters merely because they may arise in the course of the trial."

The judge went on to state:

"40. Nor would Mr Goldberger be permitted to give expert opinion evidence at the trial. A witness of fact may sometimes be able to give opinion evidence as part of his or her account of admissible factual evidence in order to provide a full and coherent explanation and account. That is what, it would appear, Master Bowles recognised when he refused the first Defendant's application to adduce expert evidence on market practice. It is what the first Defendant has done in his witness statements. Mr Goldberger, however, has expressed his opinions on market practice by way of commentary on facts of which he has no direct knowledge and of which he cannot give direct evidence. In that respect he is purporting to act exactly like an expert witness giving opinion evidence. Permission for such expert evidence has, however, been expressly refused.

41. I recognise, of course, that these rules as to witness statements and their contents are not rigid statutes. It is conceivable that in particular circumstances they may properly be relaxed in order to achieve the Overriding Objective in CPR r.1 of dealing with cases justly. I can see no good reason, however, why they should not apply to Mr Goldberger's witness statement in the present proceedings."

Fred Groves v. Used Cars Ltd

Fred Groves brings a claim against Used Cars Ltd for allegedly selling him a vehicle that was not of satisfactory quality. An employee, James Earshot, makes a statement on behalf of Used Cars Ltd.

I have read the claim by Mr Groves that Used Cars Ltd sold him a car which was not of satisfactory quality. This claim is without foundation and is merely a try on to extract money from the business because he had a change of mind and wished he had bought a different model. I work for Used Cars Ltd in the finance department as finance manager. I spoke to our salesman, Mr Blogs, the day after Mr Groves had been into the showroom. He told me that Mr Groves bought the car for £25,000. It was a sports model and had only done 20,000 miles. Seven months after he bought the car, he contacted us and said that he was claiming that it was not of satisfactory quality. His claim for damages has no basis in law because of the Consumer Rights Act 2015 and also Mr Groves is not a consumer

This so called "witness statement" is about as much use as a chocolate teapot! It breaks all the rules. The statement gives opinion about the law, opinion as to the motives for bringing the claim, reports what someone told him which is hearsay and that other person (Mr Blogs) should give direct evidence of what he experienced. In fact, it appears that this person had no direct involvement whatsoever with Mr Groves and so is not in a position to give any witness evidence. I would expect the judge to give more credence to a statement that Elvis Presley is alive! However, while this statement may seem amusing, it is not so far-fetched as you might think. I have seen many examples of litigants in person producing statements of a similar nature.

A version which might be more admissible would be as follows:

> I am employed by Used Cars Ltd as a Finance Manager. I make this statement from information within my own knowledge. Where it is not, I state the source of my belief.

> Within my department, there is a sales manager, Mr Blogs, who, I am aware from seeing the invoicing, sold a vehicle to the Claimant on _____ 2016 for £25,000. On the _____ Mr Groves came back to the garage and spoke to me as I was the only person in the showroom at the time as the others were out on staff training. He said to me that he had bought the vehicle seven months ago and had numerous problems with it. I asked him to take a seat at the desk in front of me while I brought up our records of the vehicle. I asked had he been back to us with these problems. He said that he

had but I told him that according to our records, it did not appear that he contacted the garage about any issues with the vehicle since he purchased it. He then went on to say that he never really liked the vehicle because of the seating position and the way the vehicle handled. He said that he wanted to exchange the vehicle for a different model. I said that was unlikely to happen if he had simply changed his mind about the car rather than there being an actual defect with the vehicle. Before he walked off he said, *"If this stupid little garage does not change the vehicle, I will make things difficult for you with bad press and I'll ask my mechanic friend to say to say there is a defect with the steering."* Before I could respond, he got up and walked away.

The difference between the two statements is quite obvious. The first version is full of opinion and refers to what somebody told him (hearsay), not to mention the fact that it makes legal arguments. The second statement is clearly a first-person account of what he experienced directly and does not contain opinion or legal argument.

The layout of a witness statement:

The key ingredients of a witness statement are:

- The statement must be typed on one side of A4 only with a margin of 35mm.
- At the top right-hand corner of the first page there must be the following:
  - The party on whose behalf it is filed
  - The initials and surname of the maker of the statement
  - The number of the statement in relation to the maker
  - The identifying initials and number of exhibits
- The statement must contain a formal heading with the title of the proceedings
- The body of the witness statement contains the evidence of the witness which should be in their own words and expressed in the first person.

- Statement of truth – a witness statement must contain a the bottom a "statement of truth". The wording of the statement of truth has changed since the last edition of this book. The wording is, *"I believe that the facts stated in this witness statement are true. I understand that proceedings for contempt of court may be brought against anyone who makes, or causes to be made, a false statement in a document verified by a statement of truth without an honest belief in its truth."*

It is important to emphasize the importance of the statement. By signing a statement of truth, you are confirming that the facts in the document are true. If you sign a statement of truth knowing that the documents contain false information, you could be in contempt of court. So, the signing of a statement of truth is important and the contents of the document you are signing should be checked very carefully.

At the end of this chapter is a sample witness statement in the matter of "**Esoft Ltd v. WHS Residential Properties Ltd**" to show how a statement should be set out.

Complying with directions and extensions

The above "directions" are steps that a court has ordered the parties to take to prepare for trial. It is vital that you comply with the dates stated in the order. So for example, if you do not serve your witness statements on the other party by the date in the order, you will not be able to have that oral evidence presented at trial. The rules allow the parties to agree an extension of time, but only up to 28 days. If you wish to extend the deadline beyond 28 days, you will need to make an application to the court. Even if the other party consents to the further extension, you will still need to make an application by consent to the court and pay a court fee. If you believe you are not going to be able to comply with a deadline stated in a directions order, you should make the application before the deadline expires. By making the application before the date has passed, the court should be more willing to grant the extension of time. If the deadline has already passed, the application will be one of "relief from sanctions". It is so called because failing to meet a deadline carries a sanction. In the case of witness statements, as has been said, the court can refuse to hear oral evidence from witnesses if they have not served signed statements.

If you find yourself in the position of having to apply for relief from sanctions, in addition to having to pay a court fee, you will need to have a good reason why you were late complying with the direction. The court will look at how serious the breach is, the reasons for late compliance and all the circumstances. It is not sufficient to say that there is no prejudice caused to the other side by being late. Recent cases have stated that an application for relief from sanctions can be refused where there is no prejudice to the other side. This may seem harsh but what is clear now with civil claims is that procedure plays an important role and failure to comply with procedure can mean you losing a case that has merit. It may be that this strict approach is unfair and at times in conflict with the overriding objective in Part 1 of the Civil Procedure Rules, but that is the way the wind is currently blowing from the policy makers. The harsher approach is probably linked to the limited resources of the court system and so if cases are struck out for failing to comply with the rules then that will save court time and money.

The stricter approach to case management and deadlines means that Claimants should have their documents for disclosure and witness statements all prepared (or nearly prepared) before you issue court proceedings. It will move forwards (sometimes very slowly in the early stages) but forward it will move and if you do not do something at the right point, your case is in danger of being struck out and you face a big costs bill from the other side. If you can be in the situation of having everything ready before issuing, you will put an enormous amount of pressure on the Defendant. They could seek extensions of time but that would incur court fees. If you as the Claimant have everything prepared in advance you can keep the pressure on the Defendant by only agreeing short extensions. So for example, if the Defendant is seeking to agree an extension of 28 days, you might perhaps only agree 14 days.

Where a deadline has passed, the key to an application for relief from sanctions is in the reason for the late compliance and the impact the late compliance may have on any trial date that has been set. Recent cases suggest that courts are very reluctant to allow anything to interfere with a trial date. So, if your application for an extension of time is likely to affect the trial date then it is unlikely to succeed. The strictness with which the courts are applying the rules will have an impact on litigants in person who are deliberately trying to drag out a matter. So a litigant in person who is playing games and trying to seek an adjournment of a trial date is up against it. If a trial date is adjourned then much is made of the fact that you have deprived other court users of having their time in court. This is very important in the current climate where county courts have had their budgets severely restricted and the time in court before a judge is therefore particularly valuable.

You might wonder what would be a good reason for failing to comply with a court deadline? It obviously depends on all the circumstances of a case but it is difficult to say with certainty that anything short of a sudden and serious illness preventing a party from doing a procedural step or attending court is likely to be accepted by a court. If a litigant in person was genuinely ill and could not deal with a procedural step, that would be a good reason for asking for relief from sanctions. However, the medical evidence will have to be quite specific as to why they were not able to complete the specific step, such as serving a signed witness statement. Where you have a lawyer acting it would be more difficult to persuade a court that the illness of a lawyer has prevented a step being taken on time. The reason for this is that law firms are supposed to have contingency plans in place to cope when unexpected things happen and another lawyer in the firm should be able to pick up the matter and deal with it.

If you are trying to adjourn a court hearing on medical grounds then a simple sick note from a GP is not likely to be enough. A sick note saying that you are unfit for work is not the same as a note saying that you are not fit to attend court. You may be unwell for work but you could still be expected to attend court. The court will expect the medical evidence to contain certain specific things and not simply a vague statement about being unwell. The doctor would need to specify that they attended you, how long they have been treating you, what it is about the illness which makes you unable to attend court and whether or not you could attend if reasonable adjustments were made at court. A court can make reasonable adjustments if a party is unwell by allowing, for example, regular breaks. What is clear is that courts will not allow litigants to play silly games and seek adjournments without a very good reason such as medical evidence that you are unfit to attend court.

Preparing for trial – trial bundle

If you are the claimant it is normally your job to prepare the trial bundle. If the defendant has legal representation, you could see if they will assist in its preparation. The defendant might think why should they incur the costs but actually they would benefit from a properly prepared bundle. If the defendant does not assist, or is not legally represented, you will need to know what should go in the trial bundle. The first thing to do is to come up with a draft index of the bundle and send this to the defendant about 2 to 3 weeks before the hearing. The court directions will usually expect the trial bundle to be delivered to the court seven days before the trial. By sending the draft index of the bundle to the defendant 3 weeks before the trial, that should give you enough time to hopefully agree the contents of the bundle. If you cannot agree on certain documents, there should be a section containing those documents which you cannot agree on. At the start of the trial, the dispute about these documents can be raised with the judge. There is guidance in the court rules as to what should go in the trial bundle.

Practice Direction 39 states:

Bundles of documents for hearings or trial

3.1 Unless the court orders otherwise, the claimant must file the trial bundle not more than 7 days and not less than 3 days before the start of the trial.

3.2 Unless the court orders otherwise, the trial bundle should include a copy of:

(1) the claim form and all statements of case,

(2) a case summary and/or chronology where appropriate,

(3) requests for further information and responses to the requests,

(4) all witness statements to be relied on as evidence,

(5) any witness summaries,

(6) any notices of intention to rely on hearsay evidence under rule 32.2,

(7) any notices of intention to rely on evidence (such as a plan, photograph etc.) under rule 33.6 which is not –

(a) contained in a witness statement, affidavit or experts report,

(b) being given orally at trial,

(c) hearsay evidence under rule 33.2,

(8) any medical reports and responses to them,

(9) any experts' reports and responses to them,

(10) any order giving directions as to the conduct of the trial, and

(11) any other necessary documents.

3.3 The originals of the documents contained in the trial bundle, together with copies of any other court orders should be available at the trial.

3.4 The preparation and production of the trial bundle, even where it is delegated to another person, is the responsibility of the legal representative who has conduct of the claim on behalf of the claimant

3.5 The trial bundle should be paginated (continuously) throughout, and indexed with a description of each document and the page number. Where the total number of pages is more than 100, numbered dividers should be placed at intervals between groups of documents.

3.6 The bundle should normally be contained in a ring binder or lever arch file. Where more than one bundle is supplied, they should be clearly distinguishable, for example, by different colours or letters. If there are numerous bundles, a core bundle should be prepared containing the core documents essential to the proceedings, with references to the supplementary documents in the other bundles.

Once you have agreed the contents of the trial bundle, you need to paginate it. If you have a large bundle, handwriting the page numbers does not look very tidy. If you have a scanner, preferably one with a feeder, then a good way to paginate the bundle is to scan all the documents into a PDF document and then use software which allows you to add headers and footers. You can find free software on the Internet which allows you to insert the page numbers into a PDF document. Where there is more than a hundred pages in the bundle, which is likely to be the case if the trial is not a small claims hearing, then the bundle needs to be divided with tabs with groups of relevant documents together. This means that you should have various tabs placed at appropriate points in the bundle. For example:

Tab. No.	Description	Page Number(s)
1.	Claim Form	1 to 2
	Defence	3 to 6
	Reply to Defence	7 to 9
2.	Claimant's List of Documents	10 to 14
	Defendant's List of Documents	15 to 19

Once you have prepared the trial bundle, you will need to make sufficient copies. There will need to be a copy for the judge, a copy for the defendant and a copy for witnesses. Check that each bundle is identical as there is nothing more embarrassing than getting to court only to discover that the judge's bundle does not match the other copies.

Preparing an electronic bundle

With the increased use of remote hearings, there has been a rise in court directions requiring electronic bundles to be provided to the court for the trial. General guidance has been given on how to prepare an electronic bundle:

1. *E-bundles must be provided in pdf format.*
2. *All pages in an e-bundle must be numbered by computer-generated numbering, not by hand. The numbering should start at page 1 for the first page of the bundle (whether or not that is part of an index) and the numbering must follow sequentially to the last page of the bundle, so that the pagination matches the*

     pdf numbering. If a hard copy of the bundle is produced, the pagination must match the e-bundle.

3.   *Each entry in the index must be hyperlinked to the indexed document. All significant documents and all sections in bundles must be bookmarked for ease of navigation, with a short description as the bookmark. The bookmark should contain the page number of the document.*

4.   *All pages in an e-bundle that contain typed text must be subject to OCR (optical character recognition) if they have not been created directly as electronic text documents. This makes it easier to search for text, to highlight parts of a page, and to copy text from the bundle.*

5.   *Any page that has been created in landscape orientation should appear in that orientation so that it can be read from left to right. No page should appear upside down.*

6.   *The default view for all pages should be 100%.*

7.   *If a core bundle is required, then a PDF core bundle should be produced complying with the same requirements as a paper bundle.*

8.   *Thought should be given to the number of bundles required. It is usually better to have a single hearing e-bundle and (where appropriate) a separate single authorities e-bundle (compiled in accordance with these requirements), rather than multiple bundles (and follow any applicable court specific guidance – see e.g. CPR PD52C Section VII (external link, opens in a new tab).*

9.   *The resolution of the bundle should not be greater than 300 dpi, in order to avoid slow scrolling or rendering. The bundle should be electronically optimised so as to ensure that the file size is not larger than necessary.*

10.   *If a bundle is to be added to after it has been transmitted to the judge, then new pages should be added at the end of the bundle (and paginated accordingly). An enquiry should be made of the court as to the best way of providing the additional material. Subject to any different direction, the judge should be provided with both (a) the new section and, separately, (b) the revised bundle. This is because the judge may have already marked up the original bundle.*

Summary

Court action may be viewed by many litigants in person as a long and drawn out process. The process has in recent years become longer due to a number of factors including pre-action protocols and the expectation of Alternative Dispute Resolution (such as mediation and the fact that the courts are severely underfunded and there is simply not enough court time and administrative support.

The usual stages of a court action are:

1. Pre-action protocol stage
2. Alternative Dispute Resolution
3. Issuing of proceedings
4. Filing of a defence
5. Allocation to a track with directions
6. Disclosure
7. Expert evidence if needed
8. Witness statements
9. Case management conference (in multi-track cases)
10. Pre-trial review (in multi-track cases)
11. The Trial

See opposite for sample witness statement.

On behalf of Claimant: 1st
Deponent: C Smith
Exhibits: CS
Date: 1 October 2023

IN THE COUNTY COURT AT UPTON

Between

Esoft Ltd

And

WHS Residential Properties Ltd

Case No. C05YY122

Claimant

Defendant

Statement of Chris Smith

I Chris Smith of Esoft Ltd, 39 Church Street, Upton, will say as follows:

1. I make this statement from information within my own knowledge. Where it is not I state the source of my belief. I make this statement in support of the Application for Summary Judgment.

2. I will refer to a Bundle of documents marked "CS".

3. I am a Sales Director at Esoft Ltd. I have had involvement with this matter and so I am in a position to make this statement as I am aware of the facts in this case.

4. On the 8 February 2023, Bob Green and I attended the offices of WHS and provided a full demonstration of the software product. At this meeting was Frances Bacon who I was informed does the accounts for WHS and she said that she was making the decision about whether to proceed with this software. The other intended users of the product were present. The Managing Director of WHS (Brian Brown), although not actually present in the meeting was in an adjoining room during our demonstration. I am aware that WHS had a previous demonstration of the product by Esoft.

1

5. Following the visit to their offices on 8 February, I e-mailed to Frances the proposal along with the system requirements. These are attached at pages 1-2 of the Bundle. Within the proposal at page 2 of the Bundle it refers to "Terms and Conditions" and it stated on this page that, *"All Software and Services are provided and delivered on the basis of Esoft Ltd's standard terms and conditions. A copy is available at the customer's request".*

6. On the 25 February 2023, I sent the following e-mail to Frances:

> *Hi Frances,*
>
> *Hope you are well,*
>
> *With you planning to discuss the system today with your Director, I just wanted to say that if you require anything please give me a call. I have a meeting later in the afternoon however if there are any outstanding questions I'll be available up to 1:30pm.*
>
> *It would be great to be able to obtain your commitment to this process and make use of the £2000 discount I had managed to get agreed for February.*
>
> *Kind regards,*
>
> *Chris Smith*
> *Sales Director*
> *Esoft Limited*
>
> *Tel: 0945 080 4000*
> *Mobile: 07585 550328*
>
> *Email: csmith@Esoft.co.uk*
> *Website: http://www.Esoft.co.uk*

7. On the 26 February 2023, I attended the offices of WHS and met with Frances Bacon to see if they had decided about going ahead. She said she would need to speak to the MD who I notice was in the adjoining office. I left the Agreement with Frances and went to lunch so that they could consider it. When I returned after lunch the Agreement had been signed. The signed Agreement is at page 3 of the Bundle. The Agreement states that it is subject to Esoft's standard terms and conditions, a copy of which is available at the customer's request.

8. On the 26 February 2023, a download link was sent by e-mail. A copy of this e-mail is at page 4 of the Bundle. The download link enables a customer to download software that will enable the setup of the product. We do have clients who download the software but

2

instruct other companies to set it up. An invoice was sent to WHS from our accounts department on 29 February 2023 and a copy of this is at page 5 of the Bundle. The signed Agreement makes clear that the sum of £12,000 is due on Order.

9. On 10 March 2023, I was pressed by my colleagues in accounts as to why the invoice had not been paid. I sent an e-mail to Frances, which is at page 6 of the Bundle. I asked our accounts team to allow payment by 29 March 2023 and I arranged for Bob Green to attend a session on 24th March. Following that session, I had a conversation with Frances Bacon and she stated everything was fine. I was therefore surprised that I received a telephone call on 29 March 2023 and an e-mail on 31 March 2023, which are at page 7 of the Bundle. As can be seen, that e-mail acknowledges a signed agreement but does not give any reason for cancelling apart from saying why should they pay for something they have not received.

10. It is explained in the correspondence that under Clause 6.5 of the Terms and Conditions, written notice of cancellation will not generate any refund of the annual charges for the use of the software and any payment that is outstanding shall immediately become due. On the e-mail of 31 March cancelling the Agreement the amount of £12,000 on the invoice dated 29 February 2016 became immediately due.

11. In a letter from their solicitors, Mason and Partners Solicitors, dated 24 May 2023 they state the reasons why they dispute the claim for £12,000 as being:

    1. The invoice never became due.
    2. Dispute the downlink constitutes delivery and as the software was not installed there was no sale of goods.
    3. The payment was a part payment for services to be rendered not a deposit.
    4. The Terms and Clause 6.5 was incorporated into the contract.
    5. Clause 6.5 was unfair.

12. I responded to these points in correspondence dated 25 May 2023 which is at page 16 of the Bundle. I would comment that the sum claimed is for software and licences. The Agreement makes clear that the professional services for the implementation are payable as delivered.

3

13. Following the issuing of the court claim, I have read the Defence filed by WHS. The Defence now includes arguments that were not raised in correspondence before court action was started. They now seem to also be arguing that Frances Bacon did not have authority to sign the Agreement. There is also mention that the product was "not fit for purpose". There is no mention of a specific purpose. There is only reference to them requiring it for 5 users and the "Investment Summary" in the proposal refers to 5 users. There is also mention that they did not have the opportunity to find out if it met their business needs but they had a demonstration on 8 February and we provided a detailed summary of what was identified as their requirements in the proposal sent on 9 February 2023. If they believe the product did not meet their requirements or that we had misrepresented some aspect, then it is reasonable to say that it would have been mentioned in the e-mail of cancellation dated 31 March.

14. On the 4 July 2023, I received an e-mail from Brian Brown who is the MD of WHS. That e-mail, at page 18 of the Bundle, states:

> *"We are small company and we work with good intentions, we cannot however pay for a product that does not suit our business needs. Obviously, when investing in a package such as this, the idea is that the package returns the company investment over time providing a product that works within the current business model and provides a cost effective solution. For our business at this time your system does not."*

WHS did not say that there was a particular function they wanted the software to do which it could not do. The above comment from the e-mail of 4 July 2023 supports the view that they changed their mind about the product because of financial reasons and not whether the product was fit for purpose.

15. Shortly afterwards on 7 July, I received a telephone call from Brian Brown. He said that the system *"would not be right for them"*. He then made a suggestion that they may be able to use E-Accounts and our "Lite" version of the product instead.

Summary

16. WHS signed an Agreement following our demonstration and the sending of a detailed proposal. They cancelled the Agreement by an e-mail which merely stated that they did not

4

see why they should pay £10,200 for something which they had not received. Then, when pressed for payment by solicitors, they refer to the terms of the contract not being incorporated into the contract although in that respect it was made clear on two occasions before signing the agreement that the standard terms and conditions of Esoft Ltd were available on request. Then as court action was commenced they say that Frances Bacon had no authority to sign the Agreement despite her telling me she was the one deciding whether to proceed with ordering the Software. This was not raised in correspondence from their solicitors. Further, in e-mail correspondence after court action was issued, there is mention by the MD for WHS that it was not *"fit for purpose"* but goes on say that the product does not work within *"the current business model"*.

17. In light of the above and the information contained in the Particulars of Claim, I ask the court to grant Summary Judgment as I do not believe the Defendant has real prospect of successfully defending this claim.

STATEMENT OF TRUTH

I believe that the facts stated in this witness statement are true. I understand that proceedings for contempt of court may be brought against anyone who makes, or causes to be made, a false statement in a document verified by a statement of truth without an honest belief in its truth.

Signed   *Chris Smith*

Name   CHRIS SMITH

Position   SALES DIRECTOR

Date   1 October 2023

5

Chapter 4

Small claims, Fast track or Multi track?

After the issue of a claim, the Defendant has a number of possible ways to reply. They can either:

1. Admit the claim
2. Admit part of the claim
3. Dispute the claim.

If a Defendant does nothing within the required time, then the Claimant can request a judgment in default of a response. If the claim is disputed, then it gets allocated to one of the three tracks (small, fast or multi track) depending on the size and nature of the claim. This chapter will take you through step by step examples of a defended claim in each of the tracks.

Small claims track:

Civil Procedure Rule 26 provides the scope of each track. The extent of the small claims track is described in CPR Part 26.6. A claim for a remedy for harassment or unlawful eviction relating, in either case, to residential premises shall not be allocated to the small claims track whatever the financial value of the claim. Otherwise, the small claims track will be the normal track for –

- *any claim which has a financial value of not more than £10,000 subject to the special provisions about claims for personal injuries and housing disrepair claims;*
- *any claim for personal injuries which has a financial value of not more than £10,000 where the claim for damages for*

personal injuries is not more than the relevant value specified in rule 26.6(1)(a)(ii)(aa), (bb) or (cc), being £5,000, £1,000 or £1,500, respectively; and

- *any claim which includes a claim by a tenant of residential premises against his landlord for repairs or other work to the premises where the estimated cost of the repairs or other work is not more than £1,000 and the financial value of any other claim for damages is not more than £1,000*

In general terms, a defended claim is where the amount in dispute does not exceed £10,000. To many individuals and small businesses, £10,000 is not a small sum of money, but in legal terms it is not significant.

If you bring a claim for a sum of money that does not exceed £10,000 and the defendant enters a defence, then you will receive a directions questionnaire on form N180 to complete and return to the court. The latest form N180 is shown below. The suggested information that is needed on this form is as follows:

Form N180   Small Claims Directions Questionnaire:

Section A
Mediation/Settlement

If both parties agree that the claim can be referred to mediation, then the small claims mediation service will contact you to arrange a telephone mediation. In my view the phrase "mediation" in respect of this service provided by this government body is a little misleading. All it amounts to is a conversation with a mediator who asks you for a short summary of the case and whether you have any offers to make to the other side. Making offers to settle, if that is what you wish to do, is something that most parties are capable of doing for themselves.

Directions questionnaire
(Small Claims Track)

In the	Claim No.

To be completed by, or on behalf of,

who is [1st][2nd][3rd][ ][Claimant][Defendant][Part 20 claimant] in this claim

You should note the date by which this questionnaire must be returned and the name of the court it should be returned to since this may be different from the court where the proceedings were issued.

If you have settled this claim (or if you settle it on a future date) and do not need to have it heard or tried, you must let the court know immediately.

A Settlement/Mediation

Under the Civil Procedure Rules parties should make every effort to settle their case. At this stage you should still think about whether you and the other party(ies) can settle your dispute without going to a hearing.

You may seek to settle the claim either by direct discussion or negotiation with the other party or by mediation. If settlement is reached parties may enter into a binding agreement which can be enforced if the terms of the agreement were to be breached.

Mediation is a way of resolving disputes without a court hearing, where the parties are assisted in resolving their dispute with the help of an impartial mediator. If the claim is settled at this stage the parties can avoid further court fees, costs and time involved in preparing and attending a hearing.

You may use any mediation provider. However, HMCTS provide a **free confidential** Small Claims Mediation Service which is available to parties in most small claims cases which are for less than £10,000.

Mediation is usually carried out by telephone in one hour time limited appointments convenient to the parties and is quicker than waiting for a court hearing before a judge. There is no obligation to use the Small Claims Mediation Service nor are you required to settle if you do. If you are unable to reach agreement with the other party at mediation, the claim will proceed to a small claims hearing.

You can get more information about mediation from www.gov.uk

If all parties agree, this case will be referred to the Small Claims Mediation Service. In any event the court may order the service to contact you to explore mediation.

A1 Do you agree to this case being referred to the Small Claims Mediation Service? ☐ Yes ☐ No

Please give your contact details below – If all parties agree to mediation your details will be passed to the small claims mediation team who will contact you to arrange an appointment.

You must complete the remainder of the form regardless of your answer to A1

B Your contact details

Your full name

Address for Service

Telephone number | Mobile

Email

Notes

It is essential that you provide this information, particularly if you have requested mediation. Staff will contact you within office hours (9am - 5pm).

C Track

C1 Do you agree that the small claims track is the appropriate track for this case?

☐ Yes   ☐ No

If No, say why not and state the track to which you believe it should be allocated

Track
The small claims track – generally for lower value and less complex claims with a value under £10,000. You can get more information by reading leaflet EX306 'The small claims track in civil courts'. You can get this leaflet online from hmctsformfinder.justice.gov.uk

D Suitability for determination without a hearing

D1 Do you consider that this claim is suitable for determination without a hearing, i.e. by a judge reading and considering the case papers, witness statements and other documents filed by the parties, making a decision, and giving a note of reasons for that decision?

☐ Yes   ☐ No

If No, please state why not.

The court can determine this claim without a hearing: (a) if both parties agree; or (b) where the 'Small Claims Paper Determination Pilot' applies, even if the parties do not agree. For more information on the courts participating in the pilot and the cases to which the pilot may and may not apply, please see Practice Direction 51ZC to CPR 51.

Relevant reasons include that there are factual disputes which will need the judge to hear from witnesses directly (in which case please specify the factual dispute and the relevant witnesses) or that the issues are so complex they need to be argued orally.

E About the hearing

Hearing venue

E1 At which County Court hearing centre would you prefer the small claims hearing to take place and why?

Expert evidence

E2 Are you asking for the court's permission to use the written evidence of an expert? ☐ Yes ☐ No

If Yes, state why and give the name of the expert (if known) and the area of expertise and the likely cost if appointed.

Witnesses

E3 How many witnesses, including yourself, will give evidence on your behalf at the hearing?

Hearing

E4 Are there any days within the next six months when you, an expert or a witness will not be able to attend court for the hearing? ☐ Yes ☐ No

If Yes, please give details

	Dates **not available**
Yourself	
Expert	
Other essential witness	

Will you be using an interpreter at the hearing either for yourself or for a witness? ☐ Yes ☐ No

If Yes, please specify the type of interpreter

E5 Do you believe you, or a witness who will give evidence on your behalf, are vulnerable in any way which the court needs to consider? ☐ Yes ☐ No

If Yes, please explain in what way you or the witness are vulnerable and what steps, support or adjustments you wish the court and the judge to consider.

Location
If your claim is a designated money claim the case will usually be transferred to the claimants preferred court or the defendants home court as appropriate. However, there is no guarantee of transfer to this court. For further information see CPR Parts 3, 12, 13, 14 and 26.

Expert evidence
The court must grant you permission to use an expert witness. Your notice of allocation will tell you if permission has been granted. Please note the upper limit for experts' fees that can be recovered is £750. You can get more information by reading leaflet EX306 'The small claims track in civil courts'. You can get this leaflet online from hmctsformfinder.justice.gov.uk

Witnesses
Witnesses may be asked to give evidence by either party. The court needs to have notice that you intend to call a witness. Witness expenses for travel accommodation and loss of earning should be met by the party requesting their attendance. You can get more information by reading EX342 'Coming to a court hearing'. You can get this leaflet online from hmct formfinder.justice.gov.uk

Hearing
Dates to avoid: You should enter those dates where you, your expert or an essential witness will not be able to attend court because of a holiday or other commitments.

Interpreters: In some circumstances the court will arrange for, and meet the cost of an interpreter. If you require an interpreter, you should contact the court immediately. Further details visit our website www.justice.gov.uk under 'guidance'.

Signature

You must sign this form

[blank signature box]

[Legal representative for the][1ˢᵗ][2ⁿᵈ][3ʳᵈ][   ]
[Claimant][Defendant][Part 20 claimant]

Once you have completed this form, please return it to the court at the address shown on the form N149A - Notice of proposed allocation to Small Claims Track.

You must also send a copy of this form (N180 Directions questionnaire) to each of the other parties in this case.

Section C
Track

If you believe that the case is not suitable for the small claims track, then you can indicate which track you think it should be in and give your reasons.

Generally speaking, a claim will be allocated to a track according to the financial value of the claim. If you are arguing that the claim should not be in the small claims track, then the factors which are relevant to the allocation of a track are various and are set out in CPR 26.8. These factors include the nature of the remedy sought, the complexity of the facts, law or evidence and the views expressed by the parties. So, where the claim is within the financial limit of £10,000, you would need to argue for example that the case involves complex matters of law.

D. Suitability of determination without a hearing

A small claim might be suitable for determination on the papers alone without a court hearing if the matter is for example an interpretation of a contract. In such circumstances there is little or no need to hear oral evidence from witnesses.

E1. Hearing Venue

If the defendant is an individual, then the case is normally heard in their local county court hearing centre. If you do not agree with the case being heard at the particular county court or you believe the case should be heard at a particular court, then you should state your reasons on the directions questionnaire.

E2. Expert Evidence

To be able to use expert evidence in any court hearing you have to have the permission of the court. An example of where you may need expert evidence is for example a case about a defective product and you need the expert to say what caused the defect. In small claims the district judges are less inclined to give permission to have expert evidence because they take on board the issue of proportionality. This means that it would not always be proportional to have an expert, where the case in monetary terms is relatively small compared to the cost of an expert. The winning party in a small claim can claim up to £750 towards the cost of an expert.

E3. Witnesses

When you state the number of witnesses you have to remember that yourself as a party needs to be counted as a witness.

E4: Hearing

In this section you need to state whether you have any dates which yourself or another important witness cannot attend a court hearing. The court will try to avoid these dates if possible.

E5. Vulnerable witnesses

There have been amendments to the Civil Procedure Rules to deal with vulnerable witnesses. Practice Direction 1A says:

1. *The overriding objective requires that, in order to deal with a case justly, the court should ensure, so far as practicable, that the parties are on an equal footing and can participate fully in proceedings, and that parties and witnesses can give their best evidence. The parties are required to help the court to further the overriding objective at all stages of civil proceedings.*

2. *Vulnerability of a party or witness may impede participation and also diminish the quality of evidence. The court should take all proportionate measures to address these issues in every case.*

3. *A person should be considered as vulnerable when a factor – which could be personal or situational, permanent or temporary – may adversely affect their participation in proceedings or the giving of evidence.*

So, if you think you or another witness may be vulnerable, you should raise it on the Directions Questionnaire.

The final page of the form N180 is where you sign the form. There is space below the signature where it is a good practice to state additional information which you think might assist the District Judge in giving appropriate directions. You may wish to state for example an appropriate time estimate for the small claims hearing. Generally, a small claim receives a time estimate of 90 mins to 2 hours.

Fast Track claims

Part 26.6(5) of Civil Procedure Rules describes the extent of the "Fast Track" as follows:

(4) Subject to paragraph (5), the fast track is the normal track for any claim –

(a) for which the small claims track is not the normal track; and

(b) which has a value –

(i) for proceedings issued on or after 6th April 2009, of not more than £25,000; and

(ii) for proceedings issued before 6th April 2009, of not more than £15,000.

(5) The fast track is the normal track for the claims referred to in paragraph (4) only if the court considers that –

(a) the trial is likely to last for no longer than one day; and

(b) oral expert evidence at trial will be limited to–

(i) one expert per party in relation to any expert field; and

(ii) expert evidence in two expert fields.

So generally fast track claims will be those claims that have a monetary value that exceed £10,000 but do not exceed £25,000, and the trial will take no longer than one day. When you think of "one day", in trial time that is 5 hours. Therefore, fast track cases will not normally have too many witnesses or lengthy evidence.

Multi-track claims

The multi-track is the normal track for any claim for which the small claims track or the fast track is not the normal track. In general terms, the multi-track is for claims with a value of over £25,000.

If the court believes that a claim is likely to be allocated to either the fast track or multi track, upon the receipt of a defence, it will send out form N181 to the parties. A blank form N181 is shown below. It is important to go through each section and set out how it should be completed.

A. Settlement

In this part, most parties say that they want to try to settle the case at this stage. If you state "No" then you need to come up with a good reason in the box on the form (see p.73).

B. Court

You can state which County Court you would prefer to have the case heard at. Remember, if the Defendant is an individual then it will normally be heard in their home court.

C. Pre-Action protocols

This is where you need to confirm that you complied with the pre-action protocols which usually requires the sending of a particular Letter of Claim and/or following of any other process before issuing proceedings.

D. Case Management information

You need to indicate at D1 if you intend to make an application. An example of this might be that you are going to make an application for summary judgment. At D2, you should indicate if you think the claim should be in another track such as the fast track. D3 and D4 relate to disclosure and only apply where the case is for the multi-track. At D3, you need to say if there are likely to be issues regarding the disclosure of "electronic documents". D4 deals with "non electronic documents" and it may well be that standard disclosure is the appropriate form of disclosure (see Chapter 3).

E. Experts

If an expert is needed in the case, then you should state who you intend to instruct and give the name and area of expertise for the expert, as well as the justification for using the expert and their estimated costs.

F. Witnesses

You need to list the names of the witnesses you intend to call to give oral evidence and describe which facts they will evidence on.

G. Trial or Final Hearing

This is where you indicate how long you think the trial will last. If the case is going to be in the multi-track, then it will normally last longer than one day. When putting down an estimate, it is always preferable to go for a longer estimate than a shorter one. The reason being, for example, is that if a trial is going to struggle to be completed in say two days, then better to say 3 days because otherwise the case will go what is called "part heard" and could take a long time to come back to court to be completed.

Directions

Form N181 requires you to send draft directions. You should attempt to try and agree directions with the other side as it may be that they are thinking along the same lines as you and matters can be agreed. With a fast track claim the directions are fairly standard in most cases. With a multi-track case it is quite likely that a case management conference will be listed at which the district judge will consider what directions are necessary. If a party is legally represented then they probably will be required to file a costs budget. Litigants in person are required to file a costs budget. If a costs budget is to be considered, then it will be listed as a "costs and case management conference". It has been stated by the Civil Procedure Rules Committee at the Ministry of Justice that cost budgeting will be phased out for lower value cases. November 2022 was the date when fixed costs were due to be introduced for claims up to £100,000 but this was pushed back to October 2023. The removal of costs budgeting will be a relief to lawyers as costs budgeting has been a complete waste of court time. The removal of costs budgeting should be of interest to Litigants in person because it might reduce the backlog of cases as it would free up more Judicial time.

Directions questionnaire
(Fast track and Multi-track)

In the	Claim No.

To be completed by, or on behalf of,

who is [1st][2nd][3rd][   ][Claimant][Defendant][Part 20 claimant] in this claim

You should note the date by which this questionnaire must be returned and the name of the court it should be returned to since this may be different from the court where the proceedings were issued.

If you have settled this claim (or if you settle it on a future date) and do not need to have it heard or tried, you must let the court know immediately.

If the claim is not settled, a judge will allocate it to an appropriate case management track. To help the judge choose the most just and cost-effective track, you must now complete the directions questionnaire.

You should write the claim number on any other documents you send with your directions questionnaire. Please ensure they are firmly attached to it.

A Settlement

Notes

Under the Civil Procedure Rules parties should make every effort to settle their case before the hearing. This could be by discussion or negotiation (such as a roundtable meeting or settlement conference) or by a more formal process such as mediation. The court will want to know what steps have been taken. Settling the case early can save costs, including court hearing fees.

For legal representatives only

I confirm that I have explained to my client the need to try to settle; the options available; and the possibility of costs sanctions if they refuse to try to settle.

☐ I confirm

For all

Your answers to these questions may be considered by the court when it deals with the questions of costs: see Civil Procedure Rules Part 44.

1. Given that the rules require you to try to settle the claim before the hearing, do you want to attempt to settle at this stage?

   ☐ Yes   ☐ No

2. If Yes, do you want a one month stay?

   ☐ Yes   ☐ No

3. If you answered 'No' to question 1, please state below the reasons why you consider it inappropriate to try to settle the claim at this stage.

Reasons:

The court may order a stay, whether or not all the other parties to the claim agree. Even if you are requesting a stay, you must still complete the rest of the questionnaire.

More information about mediation, the fees charged and a directory of mediation providers is available online from www.civilmediation.justice.gov.uk. This service provides members of the public and businesses with contact details for national civil and commercial mediation providers, all of whom are accredited by the Civil Mediation Council.

73

B Court

B1. (High Court only)
The claim has been issued in the High Court. Do you consider it should remain there? ☐ Yes ☐ No

If Yes, in which Division/List?

If No, in which County Court hearing centre would you prefer the case to be heard?

B2. Trial (all cases)
Is there any reason why your claim needs to be heard at a court or hearing centre? ☐ Yes ☐ No

If Yes, say which court and why?

Notes

High Court cases are usually heard at the Royal Courts of Justice or certain Civil Trial Centres. Fast or multi-track trials may be dealt with at a Civil Trial Centre or at the court where the claim is proceeding.

C Pre-action protocols

You are expected to comply fully with the relevant pre-action protocol.

Have you done so? ☐ Yes ☐ No

If you have not complied, or have only partially complied, please explain why.

Before any claim is started, the court expects you to have complied with the relevant pre-action protocol, and to have exchanged information and documents relevant to the claim to assist in settling it. To find out which protocol is relevant to your claim see: www.justice.gov.uk/guidance/courts-and-tribunals/courts/procedure-rules/civil/menus/protocol.htm

D Case management information

D1. Applications
Have you made any application(s) in this claim? ☐ Yes ☐ No

If Yes, what for? (e.g. summary judgment, add another party).

For hearing on ☐☐/☐☐/☐☐☐☐

D1. Applications
It is important for the court to know if you have already made any applications in the claim (or are about to issue one), what they are for and when they will be heard. The outcome of the applications may affect the case management directions the court gives.

D2. Track
If you have indicated in the proposed directions a track attached which would not be the normal track for the claim, please give brief reasons below for your choice.

D2. Track
The basic guide by which claims are normally allocated to a track is the amount in dispute, although other factors such as the complexity of the case will also be considered. Leaflet *EX305 – The Fast Track and the Multi-track*, explains this in greater detail.

2

D **Case management information** (continued)

D3. Disclosure of electronic documents (multi-track cases only)

If you are proposing that the claim be allocated to the multi-track:

1. Have you reached agreement, either using the Electronic Documents Questionnaire in Practice Direction 31B or otherwise, about the scope and extent of disclosure of electronic documents on each side? ☐ Yes ☐ No

2. If No, is such agreement likely? ☐ Yes ☐ No

3. If there is no agreement and no agreement is likely, what are the issues about disclosure of electronic documents which the court needs to address, and should they be dealt with at the Case Management Conference or at a separate hearing?

D4. Disclosure of non-electronic documents (all cases)

What directions are proposed for disclosure?

For all multi-track cases, except personal injury.

Have you filed and served a disclosure report (Form N263) (see Civil Procedure Rules Part 31). ☐ Yes ☐ No

Have you agreed a proposal in relation to disclosure that meets the overriding objective? ☐ Yes ☐ No

If Yes, please ensure this is contained within the proposed directions attached and specify the draft order number.

E **Experts**

Do you wish to use expert evidence at the trial or final hearing? ☐ Yes ☐ No

Have you already copied any experts' report(s) to the other party(ies)? ☐ None yet obtained

☐ Yes ☐ No

Do you consider the case suitable for a single joint expert in any field? ☐ Yes ☐ No

There is no presumption that expert evidence is necessary, or that each party will be entitled to their own expert(s). Therefore, the court requires a short explanation of your proposals with regard to expert evidence.

3

E Experts (continued)

Please list any single joint experts you propose to use and any other experts you wish to rely on.
Identify single joint experts with the initials 'SJ' after their name(s). Please provide justification of
your proposal and an estimate of costs.

Expert's name	Field of expertise (e.g. orthopaedic surgeon, surveyor, engineer)	Justification for expert and estimate of costs

F Witnesses

Which witnesses of fact do you intend to call at the trial or final hearing including, if appropriate, yourself?

Witness name	Witness to which facts

G Trial or Final Hearing

How long do you estimate the trial or final hearing will take?

☐ less than one day   ☐ one day   ☐ more than one day

☐ Hrs   ☐ State number of days

Give the best estimate you can of the time that the court
will need to decide this case. If, later you have any reason
to shorten or lengthen this estimate you should let the
court know immediately.

Are there any days within the next 12 months when you, an expert or an essential witness will not be
able to attend court for trial or final hearing?

You should only enter those dates when you, your
expert(s) or essential witnesses will not be available to
attend court because of holiday or other commitments.

If Yes, please give details

Name	Dates not available

You should notify the court immediately if any of these dates change.

4

H Costs

Do not complete this section if:

1) you do not have a legal representative acting for you

2) the case is subject to fixed costs

If your claim is likely to be allocated to the Multi-Track form Precedent H must be filed at in accordance with CPR 3.13.

I confirm Precedent H is attached. ☐

I Other information

Do you intend to make any applications in the future?   ☐ Yes   ☐ No

If Yes, what for?

In the space below, set out any other information you consider will help the judge to manage the claim.

5

77

Do you believe you, or a witness who will give evidence on your behalf, are vulnerable in any way which the court needs to consider?

☐ Yes. Please explain in what way you or the witness are vulnerable and what steps, support or adjustments you wish the court and the judge to consider.

☐ No

J Directions

You must attempt to agree proposed directions with all other parties. **Whether agreed or not a draft of the order for directions which you seek must accompany this form.**

All proposed directions for multi-track cases must be based on the directions at www.justice.gov.uk/courts/procedure-rules/civil

All proposed directions for fast track cases must be based on CPR Part 28.

Signature

Date ☐☐/☐☐/☐☐☐☐

[Legal Representative for the][1ˢᵗ][2ⁿᵈ][3ʳᵈ][   ]
[Claimant][Defendant][Part 20 claimant]

Please enter your name, reference number and full postal address including details of telephone, DX, fax or e-mail

	If applicable	
	Telephone no.	
	Fax no.	
	DX no.	
Postcode	Your ref.	

E-mail

Chapter 5

ATTENDING COURT

One of the key worries of a judge who is hearing a case conducted by litigants in person is that the trial could degenerate into some confused shambles where the rival parties have spent more time throwing insults than on the preparation of the case. To be a successful litigant in person you need to avoid the temptation of being drawn into the obsession game. It can consume some litigants in person who let it take over their lives. Every person should have the right to conduct their case in a court but you should appreciate that the courts time is valuable, especially with the limited resources provided by Government and so if you waste court time you are potentially preventing other people from having their day in court and delaying their access to justice.

Remote Court Hearings

COVID led to the court relying more on remote hearings by Zoom or Teams. During the pandemic, virtually all cases were held in this way unless there were many witnesses and it would have been difficult to conduct remotely. As restrictions imposed during COVID were eased and then removed, more hearings have returned to being in person. However, there will remain a much larger number of cases that will be heard remotely, especially small claims, applications and Tribunal cases.

If a court hearing is to be held remotely, you will normally be asked by the court to provide it with your e-mail address and telephone number in advance of the hearing. They will send you a link from which you can log on to the court hearing. It is a good idea to practice logging on by using the link the day before the hearing to check that the link is working. If it is not working, then you have time to telephone the court's technical support line to seek advice about logging on. Better to do that in good time before the hearing instead of panicking a few minutes before the scheduled hearing time when you cannot log in and you might not be able to get hold of anyone to assist. The court will want your contact telephone number as they will most likely try to call you if you have not logged in by the scheduled start time.

Having a remote court hearing poses its own issues. It will have a different feel than a court hearing in person but there are advantages such as the removal of travelling to court and waiting around in a cold and unpleasant court building. It is vital to ensure that you have a satisfactory internet connection and somewhere quiet and private at home; you do not want the children walking in during the middle of the trial as the judge will not be happy. You need to remember that all court hearings conducted online should still have the degree of formality that an in-person hearing would have. You should also dress appropriately for a remote hearing. You must avoid the temptation to record the hearing on your computer or other device that you use. Recording a court hearing is a criminal offence and this warning will be given by the judge at the start of proceedings.

The court might have asked for an electronic bundle to be provided for a remote hearing. You need to have followed the instructions for its preparation carefully by inserting bookmarks and hyperlinks as requested or appropriate. The numbering of the bundle must run from the index page. An electronic bundle was sometimes prepared so that the index was not included in the numbering. The consequence of that was that the PDF page numbers of the electronic bundle would not match the index page numbers. The court has produced guidance on how to prepare an electronic bundle (see page 53).

Although you may have prepared an electronic bundle, it is a good idea to have a paper copy of the bundle in front of you as you present your case to the court. This is because it avoids you accidentally clicking the wrong window on your screen and potentially logging yourself from the hearing and also it can prove difficult on the eyes to be staring at a screen for long periods. If you do not want to have a paper copy, then the way round this is to have two computer screens in front of you with one having the Zoom/Teams connection and the other having the electronic bundle.

Remote hearings can make it more difficult to question witnesses. Unless you have a very fast internet connection, there might be a slight delay in the witness hearing the question and you will need to take care not to talk over others. The judge will normally ask all parties online who are not talking to mute their microphones to reduce the amount of background noise. Also beware of the background behind you. You will not want others to see things behind you which you do not want them to see, and you do not want a background image that could be untidy or offensive. Best to have a background of a plain wall.

In Person Hearings

Before you leave home ensure you are dressed appropriately for court. Best to wear something that is not too flamboyant.

Before the court case, go over what you have prepared by reading it aloud. The benefit of this is to learn to project your voice. The courtroom might be a small judge's chambers or it might be a large courtroom where you will not be that close to the judge and so you will want to make yourself heard. Reading out aloud your submission to somebody else will help you gauge whether you are speaking too quickly. Speak slowly and in short sentences. The right speed will ultimately depend on the judge's reaction; the judge might want you to slow down when they are taking a detailed note.

Plan your journey to the court carefully; know where the court building is. This may sound obvious but you would not be the first to turn up at the wrong court having got the Crown Court muddled up with the County Court. If you are travelling by car, consider the nearest car park and make sure you put sufficient money on the parking meter. If you are travelling by train, allow time to find a taxi if the court building is a long way from the train station. Be prepared for your journey not to go to plan; if driving, allow plenty of time for unexpected traffic delays and if travelling by train, always take the earlier train because if a train is cancelled you might still arrive on time. It may go against your normal pattern of arriving early and hanging around, but this might be your only time in court and so for the sake of not missing it, you should be prepared to arrive early and put up with some waiting time. If things go horribly wrong and you know you are going to be late, try ringing the court office and getting a message to the usher that you are running late. If the court has other shorter cases before yours, it might put them in first.

Arriving at court

Arrive early at court . It is advisable to aim to arrive at least half an hour before the scheduled start time. When you arrive at court, be prepared to open your bags at the security desk. The security desk will not allow you take into the courtroom any object that might be used as a weapon. So, any sharp metallic object will be confiscated from you and returned to you when you leave.

Observing lawyers going into court is like watching somebody move house. They carry an incredible number of bags and trolleys. One thing you will discover is that going to court builds up your muscles as well as your stress levels. Not everything you take into court will be used but thinking of every eventuality and having a spare can save embarrassment. Before the trial you would have been required to file trial bundles. The Claimant usually has the job of preparing the trial bundle plus copies for the other side and the witness box. Having a spare copy is good practice because if you walk into the courtroom and the judge says that there is not a copy for the witness box, then to the delight of the judge you can step forward and produce your spare copy. Otherwise, a delay will ensue while a further copy is done. It might not be your fault that the bundle has not found its way to where it should be, but the judge will be very grateful that you have avoided the court wasting time.

After having been searched at the door by security, head towards the court usher and get your yourself signed in. You will also see from the usher's list whether your opponent has arrived. If they have arrived, then once you have settled yourself down, it might be appropriate to speak to them to see if they are proposing any last-minute offers to settle the case. If you have any other witnesses that are appearing to give evidence, then ensure that they have arrived and they know which courtroom the hearing is taking place in. Witnesses will normally be asked to wait outside until they are called to give their evidence.

Expect to have a long wait at court. The court will usually list several cases at the same time on the assumption that not all cases will proceed as many will settle at a late stage. This can on occasions lead to the court not being able to hear all the cases on that day due to a lack of time and your case might be the unlucky one that gets adjourned. This may not appear a very satisfactory system but with limited resources it is the method that has to be used to try and avoid empty courtrooms.

In the Courtroom

How to behave in court is a very important skill. It is not only the arguments that are important, but the way you present yourself. Many people have seen television programmes such as Judge Judy or Judge Rinder. Although these programmes are made for entertainment purposes, there are some basic lessons to learn from watching Judge Judy and the way she treats litigants who try to interrupt her. If you are before a District Judge in the County Court, knowing when to speak and when not to speak is vital. Observing whether the judge wants you to speak or realising that the judge is criticising your opponent, and so you do not need to say anything, takes practice and patience. Judge Judy may play up to the cameras to make a drama out of a situation where a litigant is trying to be clever but, if you play up in a county court (or any court for that matter) there is a strong chance the judge will become very annoyed with you and miss any good arguments you may have. As somebody once said, the first few minutes you are in a courtroom are when opinions are formed. To a large degree you can tell which way things are going from very early on in proceedings. You therefore do not want to cloud the judge's impression of you (and your case) by being disruptive.

Interim Hearings and Applications

So, you may think that this chapter will only mention what to do and what to say at a final trial, it is probably worth describing what to do at interim hearings. Although the obsessed litigant in person will always think his case will go all the way to a long and dramatic trial, the chances are that the matter will suddenly and unexpectedly reach a settlement. A settlement may be brought about by a sudden moment when the realisation dawns on the litigants that they should settle because the dispute is becoming ridiculous and adverse to their health (which is often what happens in boundary disputes) or a Case Management Hearing before the trial when the judge gives a heavy hint that a party has serious difficulties and this brings forward a resolution of the case. Therefore, how to deal with interim hearings is something a litigant in person needs to be able to cope with. It needs to be remembered that interim hearings or applications are exactly that and so you should not try to conduct it like the "War of the Roses" in the 15 minutes slot the court listing officer has allocated.

Let us suppose you are applying to set aside a default judgement because you did not receive the claim form and you have a real defence to the claim. You should not saturate the court and the other party with pages of irrelevant information but simply concentrate on presenting to the district judge the fact that you have the basis to satisfy the test for setting aside a default judgement. By way of an example, consider the case of **Uptown Marketing v. Fast Communications** to illustrate what you might expect when making this type of application. In this case, Fast Communications obtained a County Court judgment against Uptown for the sum of £10,000.

Background: Uptown Marketing v. Fast Communications

Uptown Marketing is a small two-partner limited liability firm that has been trading in a rural town for many decades. The two partners, Mr Town and Mrs Well, decided to upgrade their telephone system and invited Fast Communications to provide them with a proposal. They presented a proposal for a new digital phone system along with all the lines and handsets. The cost of this new system was £12,000 and this included support for the first year. The contract said that £2,000 would be due on signing the agreement. Mr Town paid the £2,000 and Fast Communications came and installed the new phone system.

Two weeks after installation, the lines went dead. Fast Communications attended to repair the system as part of their support package. The phones worked for a further two weeks before the lines once again went dead. Fast Communications then refused to do any further repairs to the phone system as they said it would need an upgrade of the hardware as well as the software on their computer system to enable the new digital phone system to operate. Mr Town was surprised but even more shocked that Fast Communications expected him to pay for the additional equipment and for the cost of installing it. Uptown wrote letters of complaint and made it very clear that in their view they had stated before inviting Fast Communications to put forward a proposal what their system was and what they wanted the new one to do.

Fast Communications responded that they would not be providing the upgrade. They claimed that what they had installed would do what Uptown wanted but it had crashed because they were using it in a different way and had more uses than originally planned. Uptown said they would not make payment of any more instalments until the phone system was working. Uptown had to take emergency measures to save their business and so got another company to get the phone system working. Fast Communications then threatened legal action and after no payments were received, they issued a County Court claim via money claims online.

For whatever reason, Uptown said they did not receive the claim form and fast communications obtained judgement in default. However, Fast Communications did not request judgment immediately and waited 2 weeks before doing so. It was sent to the address on the claim form but that address recently ceased to be the registered office of Uptown. The judgement lay at the previous registered office for 3 weeks before being forwarded to the new registered office of Uptown. By the time the judgment arrived on the desk of Mr Town, nearly 4 weeks had passed since the judgment was entered. Both partners were about to go on two weeks annual leave and decided to deal with the matter when they returned. However, before leaving for their holiday, they instructed the office manager to write to Fast Communications to find out why they had received a court judgment without receiving any claim form and asked Fast Communications to forward a copy. Uptown then asked Fast Communications to agree to set aside the Judgment but they refused and so Uptown must make an application on Notice. On the return from their holiday, the partners made the application to the court which, by now, was nearly 7 weeks since the judgment was entered.

Uptown Marketing are acting as litigants in person and they have never been to court before. What should they say and do to ensure the best chance of getting the judgment set aside?

The application, which must be made on form N244 and will require a court fee of £255, will need to explain the basis on which they are asking the court to set aside the judgment. It will need to be supported by a short witness statement along with relevant documents. The judge will probably only see the papers shortly before the hearing and so it is vital that they clearly express in the short time they will have before the judge the key points as to why the judgment should be set aside. It is often a good idea to have sent to the court, shortly before the hearing, a skeleton argument so that the judge will have a short summary of the key facts and the issues that need to be determined. Doing so will earn favour with the judge. It will also make the job of speaking in court much easier as you have will have an outline to follow.

An application to set aside judgment should focus on whether there is a real prospect of success. The Application needs to be made promptly once you have become aware of the judgment. Setting aside a correctly entered judgment requires the defendant to show that they have a real prospect of successfully defending the claim or there is some other reason why the judgment should be set aside or varied. CPR Part 13 governs the procedure. If the judgment was entered incorrectly, then the judgment should be set aside as of right rather than at the discretion of the court. An example of where a judgment should be set aside as of right is where the claim form was not served in accordance with the rules.

In the case of Uptown **Marketing v. Fast Communications**, it appears that the Claim Form was sent to the correct address and so it seems unlikely that any issues about this are relevant to the application, apart from explaining the delay in making the application. If a claim form was sent to the correct address but simply did not arrive in the post, that is not an automatic reason for a judgment to be set aside but it may be a good reason for the judge to exercise his discretion and set it aside.

An appropriate skeleton argument for Uptown Marketing might be:

In the County Court at Uptown[2]   **Case Number**

Between

Fast Communications   **Claimant**

And

Uptown Marketing   **Defendant**

Skeleton Argument of the Defendant

----

1. This is an application by Uptown Marketing to set aside the judgement entered on xx/xx/xx

2. The court will be aware that the test for setting aside a judgment entered correctly is under CPR Part 13.3:
   - The defendant has a real prospect of successfully defending the claim or
   - There is some other good reason why judgment should be set aside or the defendant be allowed to defend the claim

3. The Claim Form, although sent to the correct address, was not received by Uptown Marketing. In the period between the Claim being issued and judgment being requested, our registered office changed and this caused a delay in Uptown becoming aware of the judgment. However, upon becoming aware of the judgment, we have acted promptly in making this application as we did so within 3 weeks of having knowledge of the judgment.

------

[2] Uptown is a fictitious place and there is no such court. However, with all the recent closures of county courts there very few left with a move to the regionalisation and centralisation of the county court system.

4. The statement of Mr Upton, attached to the Application, explains that we believe that there is a real prospect of successfully defending this claim. The basis of our defence is that we relied on the expertise of the Claimant in respect of the installation of a new telephone system. We explained to Fast Communications what equipment we had in our office and they suggested new software and a digital phone system. The new phone system would sit on our server and would operate through the broadband internet line. Two weeks after the installation of the phone system it would not work and Fast Communications said that they would not fix the problem unless we paid for an upgrade to our server.

5. We refused to pay the additional sum and any further invoices submitted by Fast Communications until they fixed the phone system. They would not agree to do that and so to keep our business functioning, we instructed another company to install what was compatible with our existing server.

6. In short, we argue that there is a real prospect of defending this claim as Fast Communications did not exercise reasonable care and skill in the service they provided as they failed to recognise and inform us that the system we had purchased from them was not compatible with the existing server. It was not for the purpose we specified.

There is a strong prospect in all the circumstances that the District Judge would set aside the judgment entered against Uptown Marketing. They can establish that they acted reasonably promptly once they became aware of the judgment. If you delay for longer than a month before making an application, then you would have more difficulty in convincing a court you acted promptly. The usual order would be to require them to file a defence within 14 days.

Conducting your case at the Trial

Normally, the Claimant will go first. As Claimant, you should start with a short opening statement unless the judge indicates they want you to move straight on to presenting the evidence. The opening statement is not meant to be like a speech at a political rally but instead a concise summary of what your case is, how you intend to prove it, and the evidence you intend to present. Explain in simple terms what you are asking the court to give you and the key reasons why. The following would be an example in a straightforward case:

> *"Sir, my claim is against Mr Blogs for a breach of contract. I paid Mr Bloggs £20,000 to build an extension to my house but he did not do the work to a reasonable standard and there were a number of defects. My claim is for the costs I have incurred to rectify the faults caused by the failure of Mr Blogs to exercise reasonable care and skill. I will be calling evidence from an expert to show that the work was not done to a satisfactory standard and will present evidence of the costs I incurred to put the defects right."*

Using simple and jargon free language is the right thing to do. Judges, contrary to what you might think from watching TV dramas, prefer you to speak in plain language and get to the point. They are always up against time constraints and do not want you to be verbose. If you assist judges in getting to the crux of a case, it will make their life easier and they can dispose of a case more quickly.

After you have made your opening statement, the other side have their chance to do the same. After that it will be your turn to present your evidence.

When it is your turn to give evidence, you will go into the witness box. You will only be able to take a copy of your signed witness statement and a copy of the agreed trial bundle. As you will be representing yourself, you will tell the court that you wish to put into evidence the statement you made on such and such a date which is at page X of the trial bundle. You will not need to read out what you said in your statement, unless you are in certain

Tribunals (such as the Employment Tribunal). The judge might ask if there is anything which you may wish to change or add to your statement. If there are any points you wish to alter then tell the judge. If you want to add anything new then you will need the permission of the judge to do so. Once that is done, then it will be the opportunity of the other side (or their lawyer) to ask you questions about your witness statement.

It is crucial to not let the questioning wind you up. You need to be familiar with your written witness statement as that will form the basis of the questioning. Stay calm and simply answer the question. It is the job of the other side's advocate (assuming they have one) to test your evidence and to do this they will put questions to you to imply that your version of events is not correct. If you get defensive or start arguing with the advocate, you will lose credibility with the judge. Simply answer the questions in an honest and straightforward manner. If you come across as being yourself, then it is much more likely that the judge will regard you as a credible witness. Not only will the judge use your demeanour to decide whose evidence is preferred, they will also listen for inconsistencies in what you have said in your evidence/statement compared with all the other evidence heard during the trial. The advocate will try to ask you a question which will cast doubt on aspects of your evidence; in doing so, they are trying to persuade the judge that, on balance, the judge will prefer the evidence of the barrister's client. This should explain that where a case depends on a finding of fact, it is very difficult to appeal the decision of a judge. Any appeal judge would say that the original trial judge is best placed to decide which set of facts is preferred. The trial judge is ideally placed to see the look on the face of witnesses when asked awkward questions. This is surely a very strong argument why online courts are not necessarily a good way to decide cases where there are disputes of fact.

Once you have presented all of your evidence at the trial, the other party will have their opportunity to put their case. You will have the chance to cross examine the witnesses of the other side. It is a very good idea to have prepared questions in advance. Ensure that they are proper questions; often in court non-lawyers end up making a speech rather than putting an actual question. The purpose of cross examination is for you to test and probe their evidence. You may wish to put questions, for example which say:

> *"I put it to you Mr Blogs that the reason the roof leaked was that you did not correctly attach the felt to the rafters?"*

The above process is described as "putting your case" to the witness. You should make careful notes of what the witness says in reply to your question so that you may refer to the evidence given when you make your closing speech.

When asking questions in cross examination, there is an old rule of thumb which many barristers subscribe to which is that you should never ask a question which you do not know the answer to or which allows the witness to say something unexpected. In reality, this mean that you should try to ask "closed questions" where there are usually only "Yes" or "No" answers. In this way, you exercise some control over what the witness says. If you ask too many open questions there is the danger that the witness will come out with something totally unexpected and you will have difficulty of thinking on your feet as to what to ask next.

Although you should not make comments on what the witness says in reply to your questions, you may want to follow up and ask them to explain to the court if it displays an inconsistency. So if Mr Blogs describes the fact that he does not accept that he incorrectly fitted the felt to the rafters because he did it in a particular way "X", but the expert report says he did not attach it in that way but used a different method called "Y", then you might wish to point out this difference to the witness and say to him in another question:

> *"Is it not the case that you are saying in your statement what you should have done but in fact the evidence of the expert is that you actually used the wrong method for fastening the material?"*

The key part of the preparation of cross examination is to identify inconsistencies in the evidence and to then ask the witnesses about the contradiction. When taking the witness to the inconsistent material in the evidence, ensure you have to hand the exact page reference so that you can quickly take the witness to the relevant section. By pointing out the inconsistencies you are effectively saying to the judge that their case does not add up and so your version of events should be preferred. As Judge Judy often says on her television show, "If it does not make sense, it's not true!" Of course, it is better to say (in your closing submission) that the evidence of the defendant (or claimant) is not credible for the reasons you have identified, and that therefore on balance the judge should prefer your version of events.

At the end of the trial, you will most likely be given the opportunity to make a closing submission. Use your closing speech as a chance to summarise your main arguments and the evidence that was presented which supports your case. It is a good idea to have sketched out in advance the outline of your closing speech and to leave gaps to put in notes from the evidence which is supportive of a particular point. If it was a relatively short hearing, it may not be necessary to go over the evidence again but with a long trial with several witnesses it will assist to summarise the bits of evidence that were presented which support each argument in your case. These closing speeches will not (or should not) be dramatic affairs as you may have seen in television dramas such as Kavanagh QC or Judge John Deed. You are not making a passionate plea for justice, but simply summarising your best arguments to the judge and highlighting the evidence that was heard or the documents in the bundle which support these submissions. In the closing speech, if you understand the points of law that are involved, you can make simple submissions about what is the legal position but do not worry if you do not have anything to say; you are not a qualified lawyer and the judge will understand that. It is better to steer clear of making many points about the legal position as there is a danger that you will distract the judge from the real issue. If the other side has a lawyer, they will be required to set out the law to the judge, explaining the points in their favour and those which support your case.

In summary, it is important to know your limits at the trial and if there is something you do not understand, then ask the judge if he could explain it. As always, preparation is the key and so carefully prepare what you intend to say in your opening statement, the questions you want to put to witnesses in cross examination and the main points you wish to cover in your closing submission. Speak slowly and keep an eye the judge. Don't get carried away and do not engage in histrionics.

The judge will either proceed to give judgment straight away or may decide to adjourn for a short period to consider the decision. In more complicated cases, the judge may decide to go away and carefully assess all the evidence that has been presented and so may "reserve" judgment and produce a decision at a later date. It might be several weeks or months before you get the judgment, but the court will contact you when the judge has made a decision. The judge may send out a written version of the judgment or may decide to ask the parties to come back to court when the judge will read out the decision. If the judge reads out the judgment (either straight after the trial or at a later date), you will need to write a careful and detailed note of what is said. This is not particularly easy to do when the judge is discussing difficult points of law but do the best you can. If the other side has a lawyer, then you could always ask them to let you have a copy of their note of the judgment. The reason why it is vital to have a good and accurate note of the judgment is so that you can make a decision as to whether you feel you may have grounds to appeal. If you instantly feel there is a basis for an appeal you should ask the judge for permission to appeal and you will be asked to briefly set out why you think there might be a basis for an appeal. It is probably better to go away and reflect on the decision and to seek a professional view as to whether you think the judge has made a mistake with regards to the law or his decision is so wrong that it is not sustainable.

Appealing

If you do not obtain permission to appeal from the lower court which heard the case, you will need to seek permission from the appropriate appeal court. You must seek permission within 21 days of the decision of the lower court. The test which the courts apply when deciding applications for permission to appeal is:

1. Does the appeal have a real prospect of success, or
2. Is there some other compelling reason why the appeal should be heard

When making the appeal, you need to use form N161 if the case was not heard in the small claims track and N164 if it was a small claim. If the appeal court rejects your application for permission on the papers, you are entitled to request within 7 days of receiving the decision, an oral hearing where you can try to persuade the court to reconsider the decision to refuse permission.

The appeal as has been stated, must be made within 21 days of the date of the decision unless the judge at the hearing granted further time for an appeal to be made or you apply for an extension of time. The grounds for an appeal are that the decision of the lower court was:

1. Wrong; or
2. Unjust because of serious procedural or other irregularity in the proceedings in the lower court

In addition, a decision will only be wrong or unjust if it would have made a difference to the decision of the lower court. An appeal cannot introduce a new point that was not made in the lower court unless there is sufficient reason.

The meaning of "wrong" is that the decision of the lower court is unsustainable. It is very difficult to argue that a decision was wrong based on a finding of fact. This is because the trial judge is best placed to assess the demeanour and credibility of witnesses than the appeal court. However, a decision may be plainly wrong on the facts if it cannot be reasonably explained or justified, meaning that no reasonable judge could have made it.

The full procedure for making an appeal is contained CPR Part 52 and Practice Direction 52. Deciding whether you have the basis for an appeal is a complex legal assessment and the litigant in person would be advised to seek a view from an experienced counsel in the particular area of law. It may be that the litigant in person could make use of a direct access barrister. Having advice from an experienced barrister is worth the money, because having lost a case it is sometimes difficult to be objective and see the other side of the argument and to understand why the judge found against you.

Summary

Attending court can be one of the most nerve-racking experiences for a litigant in person. However, with the increase in litigants in person the courts are more aware of the issues faced by them and reasonable measures are taken by the judge to ensure that a litigant in person understands what is happening at a trial. That said, there is only one set of civil procedure rules and as a litigant in person, you must be aware that the rules will be applied in the same way whether you are represented or not.

The hearing is your one opportunity to put across your case in the best possible light. Plenty of careful preparation is usually the key to presenting all the relevant points to the judge. The skill of courtroom advocacy is not to create dramatic effect but to explain your points in a clear and concise way that the judge can follow; remember the judge probably will see the papers for the first time on the day of the hearing and will find favour with someone who draws their attention to the relevant facts in a simple manner. Preparing a straightforward skeleton argument in advance is often a vital tool at a hearing where time is limited. A skeleton argument will usually be required to be prepared before the trial; a well-prepared skeleton will help the judge to see the wood from the trees before the trial gets going.

❖❖❖

Chapter 6

LANDLORD AND TENANT

There are a number of situations where a litigant in person may encounter issues relating to a tenancy. This could be a tenant who is defending possession proceedings or a landlord seeking to evict a tenant. The common situation is that of possession proceedings being brought by a landlord against the tenant who by default is occupying the premises under an assured shorthold tenancy.

Being able to understand the legal procedure and legal rights as a tenant is a valuable piece of knowledge. A landlord is more likely to have the resources to instruct solicitors to take the necessary legal measures to recover possession of their property. However, many landlords decide to act for themselves to recover possession of their property. That is not necessarily the wrong thing to do on the part of the landlord but a landlord has so many legal obligations with regard to residential tenants that they need to keep on top of the current legislation. As a landlord, there are various requirements that you must comply with, for example in relation to gas safety, and in this respect you should seek proper advice as to what you need to do to comply. The purpose of this chapter is to look at how to represent yourself as a litigant in person in a matter concerning a tenancy. We will look at the procedure which a landlord acting for him or herself must follow in order to successfully recover possession of property under an assured short hold tenancy.

Before looking at an example of a landlord trying to seek possession of an assured short hold tenancy following the service of a section 21 notice (i.e. giving the tenant two months' notice to terminate the agreement) or a section 8 notice to establish one of the grounds in schedule two of the Housing act 1988, it is important to understand a little about the obligations a landlord has and the responsibilities of a tenant. In recent years, there has been a wealth of legislation and regulations that has put more burdens on the landlord in the private sector. The following requirements are amongst the many imposed upon a landlord:

- *from 1 February 2016 landlords must undertake a document check to ensure the tenant has the right to rent in the UK*
- *the landlord at the start of the tenancy must provide the tenant information pack*
- *the landlord must comply with obligations in relation to electrical equipment, fire regulations, gas safety regulations as well as having an energy performance certificate.*
- *the landlord must ensure the property is in a safe state and in a good standard of repair*
- *if the landlord takes a deposit then the deposit must be protected in an approved scheme.*

The above are just some of the many considerations that a private landlord has to take on board when letting premises. In some situations, for example where the tenancy is for three years or more, a written tenancy agreement must be provided. It is in any situation advisable for the landlord to have a properly drafted tenancy agreement. A standard assured short hold tenancy agreement can be obtained from stationers or downloaded from the Internet. The majority of tenancies are assured short hold tenancies and these can either be for a fixed term or periodic, which means that they run from period to period such as from month to month. When a fixed term AST expires and the tenant remains in the property, the tenancy continues as a statutory periodic AST. An AST is the default tenancy where no other tenancy is created. ASTs were introduced in the Housing act of 1988 and because they provide less security of tenure for the tenant it was thought that these types of tenancies would encourage landlords to rent their properties in the private sector.

It is arguable that with the increased burden of legislation that has been imposed on landlords in recent years, it is discouraging private landlords from letting and this could have a significant impact on the availability of housing.

The tenancy agreement is important and should contain certain matters which would assist the landlord if disputes arise or they wish to later seek possession of the property. The landlord's address for service of documents should be stated in the tenancy or the address of the landlord's agent where documents can be served should be given, otherwise under the landlord and tenant act 1987 until such information is provided to the tenant rent does not accrue.

Another example of the importance of getting the tenancy agreement correctly drafted is to include a clause that if the landlord wishes to seek possession on one of the grounds in the Housing act 1988 schedule two, then the agreement must contain a statement mentioning which grounds within schedule two the landlord may seek possession on. The common grounds in schedule two which a landlord may use during a fixed term of an AST include the grounds 8, 10 and 11 which relate to some rent being due (ground 10), at least two months' rent being due (ground 8) and persistently late in paying rent (ground 11). The case of **Fred Smith v. Mr Dominic Reed** illustrates the problems faced by the landlord if the tenancy agreement does not contain the statement as to the grounds on which the landlord can seek possession:

Fred Smith v. Dominic Reed

Fred Smith entered into a tenancy agreement with Mr Reed on 10 October 2022. Mr Reed provided the tenancy agreement which he had used for many years in respect of the tenancies he had let and it was not an agreement which a lawyer had looked over. A copy of the tenancy agreement is at the end of this chapter. The tenancy was a fixed term assured shorthold tenancy agreement for 3 years, starting on 16 October 2022 with a monthly rent of £750 payable in advance on the 16th day of each month. Mr Smith starts to fall behind with his rent. Mr Reed serves a section 8 Notice based on Grounds 8 and 10 in Schedule Housing Act 1988 as amended, namely that he is at least 2 months behind with his rent and that there is some rent due. Mr Reed starts possession proceedings.

Mr Reed's claim for possession will fail because the tenancy agreement does not comply with Section 7(6) of the Housing Act 1988 as amended. This section states:

(6) The court shall not make an order for possession of a dwelling-house to take effect at a time when it is let on an assured fixed term tenancy unless—

(a) the ground for possession is Ground 2[F8, Ground 7A] [F9, Ground 7B] or Ground 8 in Part I of Schedule 2 to this Act or any of the grounds in Part II of that Schedule, other than Ground 9 or Ground 16; and

(b) the terms of the tenancy make provision for it to be brought to an end on the ground in question (whether that provision takes the form of a provision for re-entry, for forfeiture, for determination by notice or otherwise).

The tenancy agreement should have contained wording which stated that the landlord may seek possession during the fixed term if they can prove on the grounds contained in Schedule 2 of the Housing Act 1988 as amended. The wording should have stated the following:

If any of the grounds specified in Schedule 2 to the Housing Act 1988 apply, Landlord may seek to repossess the Property during the fixed term by giving the Tenant notice under section 8 of the Housing Act 1988 of his intention to apply to court for possession and, subsequently, applying to the court for a possession order.

Tenancy Deposits

The failure to comply with rules on tenancy deposits can cause problems and even prevent a landlord from seeking possession by way of serving a section 21 notice. If the landlord wishes to take a deposit at the beginning of the tenancy, then the deposit must be protected by one of the authorised schemes. The tenant must be provided with details of the scheme in which it is held and the scheme rules within 30 days. Not only does a failure to protect the deposit leave the landlord open to a claim by the tenant, but the landlord would be prevented from taking possession proceedings based on the section 21 notice until the issue is dealt with and that would normally be resolved by the landlord having to return the deposit before he is able to serve a valid section 21 notice.

A landlord also has to be aware of new laws in the deregulation act 2015 which provides safeguards to a tenant and prevents a landlord from taking possession proceedings using the section 21 notice for a period of six months if that section 21 notice was served in retaliation for a complaint about repairs at the property

Jacky Wilson v. Dominic Reed

Jacky Wilson is a tenant of Mr Reed under an AST. The AST is for an initial fixed term of 12 months. After the 12 months of the tenancy, Ms Wilson raises an issue regarding the repair to the heating system. Mr Reed acknowledges the issue within 14 days of receiving the complaint saying that he will get an engineer to look at the issue by the end of the month. Ms Wilson does not have any further communication nor is the boiler repaired. 30 days after reporting the faulty boiler, Ms Wilson receives a section 21 notice from Mr Reed. The section 21 notice gives Ms Wilson the required 2 months notice. At the end of the 2 month period, Ms Wilson receives notice of a claim for possession through the accelerated procedure. Ms Wilson defends the claim for possession on the grounds that the section 21 notice was served in retaliation for her report of a problem with the heating system. What are the prospects of Ms Wilson successfully defending the claim for possession?

What process must a tenant follow when reporting a complaint?

Tenants should always report any disrepair, or poor conditions that may arise, to the landlord as soon as possible. They should put their complaint in writing. In order to rely on the protection against retaliatory eviction that the Deregulation Act 2015 provides, a tenant must approach the landlord in the first instance. If, after 14 days from the tenant making a complaint, the landlord does not reply, that reply is inadequate, or they respond by issuing a section 21 eviction notice, the tenant should approach their local authority and ask them to step in and carry out an inspection to verify the need for a repair. The Local Authority will arrange to inspect the property and they will conduct a thorough check.

There is a detailed assessment method (known as the Housing Health and Safety Rating System) that has been developed to help Local Authorities verify whether a property contains serious health or safety hazards. If the inspection verifies the tenant's complaint, the inspector will take appropriate action. There are a number of enforcement options open to Local Authorities, including Improvement Notices and Notices of Emergency Remedial Action, but they will almost always engage with the landlord first, in order to try to resolve the problem informally. If the local authority serves an Improvement Notice or Notice of Emergency Remedial Action, the landlord cannot evict the tenant for 6 months using the no-fault eviction procedure.

If you are the tenant, and you are considering a disrepair claim, remember that there is a pre-action protocol that you would be expected to comply with. The Pre-Action Protocol contains template letters which should be used. These are very useful as they contain what needs to be covered and so it is a matter of you filling in the blanks.

Applying for possession of residential property

The procedure for possession proceedings is contained in the Civil Procedure Rules Part 55. There is an accelerated procedure which can be used following the service of a section 21 notice and the process does not usually involve a hearing and the judge will grant an order for possession based on the papers. This is a no fault process whereby the landlord only has to show that the tenancy has come to an end and the correct section 21 notice has been served. The section 21 notice will not be valid if the landlord has not complied with various statutory requirements. To take advantage of the accelerated procedure, there needs to have been a signed written tenancy agreement.

If the landlord seeks to evict a tenant based on a fault basis, such as unpaid rent or other breaches of the tenancy agreement, the landlord will have to serve a notice under section 8 and then if the tenant does not rectify the breach within 14 days, such as making payment of the rent, then the landlord can issue a claim for possession to the county court and a hearing will be listed for the case to be heard.

Completing the paperwork for a possession claim

This section explains the procedure for making a claim for possession either by using the "accelerated possession procedure" or not. It is somewhat ironic that the procedure known as accelerated possession procedure can often be anything but accelerated!

Seeking possession of an Assured Shorthold Tenancy using Accelerated Possession Procedure

At the end of this chapter, there are completed examples of:

1. Section 21 Notice
2. Claim Form for Possession - Form N5b

To start a claim for accelerated possession, you need to take or send the Claim Form (along with a copy) plus a copy of the tenancy agreement and the court fee to the County Court Hearing Centre which covers the district where the property is situated.

The Claim Form (N5b) has increased in size since the first edition of this book. It extends to many pages and so at the end of this chapter I reproduce only important extracts from it. The full form can be download from the Court Service website.

The Court will issue the Claim and send out the copy of the Claim Form to the Defendant. The Defendant will have 14 days in which to respond to the Claim. The Defendant will also be sent a copy of the "Defence Form" (N11b) to complete and return. After 14 days, the papers are referred to the judge with any Defence that might have been filed. If the judge considers the papers and is satisfied that the Claimant is entitled to possession, then an Order for possession will be made. If the judge is not satisfied, then a hearing may be listed. CPR Part 55.16 states what the options are when the judge comes to consider the Claim and any Defence.

Consideration of the claim

55.16

(1) After considering the claim and any defence, the judge will –

(a) make an order for possession under rule 55.17;

(b) where the judge is not satisfied as to any of the matters set out in paragraph (2) –

(i) direct that a date be fixed for a hearing; and

(ii) give any appropriate case management directions; or

(c) strike out the claim if the claim form discloses no reasonable grounds for bringing the claim.

(1A) If—

(a) the judge directs that a date be fixed for hearing in accordance either with paragraph (2) or rule 55.18(1); and

(b) the claim has not been brought in the County Court hearing centre which serves the address where the land is situated, the judge will direct that the proceedings should be transferred to that hearing centre.

(2) The matters referred to in paragraph (1)(b) are that –

(a) the claim form was served; and

(b) the claimant has established that he is entitled to recover possession under section 21 of the 1988 Act against the defendant.

(3) The court will give all parties not less than 14 days' notice of a hearing fixed under paragraph (1)(b)(i).

(4) Where a claim is struck out under paragraph (1)(c) –

(a) the court will serve its reasons for striking out the claim with the order; and

(b) the claimant may apply to restore the claim within 28 days after the date the order was served on him.

The reality is that if the correct procedures have been followed and the tenant has been provided with the right information at the start of the tenancy, then the judge will make an Order for possession within 14 days without having a hearing.

Date_____ 20_____

Between:

1. (Landlord)

Name_____

Address_____

Telephone Number_____

Registered office_____

Emergency telephone number_____

2. (Tenant)

Name_____

Property address:

_____

_____

Tenancy start date:

The tenancy begins on_____

and is a:

weekly / monthly / yearly tenancy at £   per week / month

And the method of payment is to be_____

Responsibility:

The landlord / tenant will be responsible for water charges, utility bills and council tax

TENANT'S OBLIGATIONS

The tenant agrees with the landlord as follows:

(a) to pay the rent as and when it falls due;

(b) to keep the interior of the premises and the fixtures, fittings, windows and other things, which form part of the premises, in as good a condition as they are in now. The tenant also agrees to make good any wilful damage that is done to the premises during the term of this tenancy;

(c) not to part with possession of the premises or sub-let the whole of the premises;

(d) to use the premises for living in as his/her only or principle home and not to operate a business at the premises without written consent from the landlord;

(e) not to cause or allow members of his/her household or visitors to cause a nuisance/annoyance to neighbours or the neighbourhood;

(f) not to commit or allow members of his household or visitors to commit any form of harassment on the grounds of race, colour, religion, sex, sexuality or disability which may interfere with the peace and comfort of, or cause offence to neighbours;

(g) not to play or allow to be played hi-fi equipment or a musical instrument so loudly that it causes a nuisance or annoyance to neighbours;

(h) not to keep pets in the premises without the landlord's consent;

(i) to keep the interior of the premises in a good/clean condition and to decorate all internal parts of the premises as frequently as is necessary to keep them in good decorative order;

(j) to undertake any necessary minor repairs to the premises i.e. changing washers on leaking pipes or attending to blocked sinks;

(k) to report to the landlord promptly any defect in or damage to the structure or internal installations of the premises;

(l) to allow the landlord or his agent/employees access at all reasonable hours of the daytime to inspect the condition of the property or to carry out repairs to the premises or adjoining property;

(m) not to assign or sub-let the tenancy and take in lodgers without the landlord's written consent;

(n) to give the landlord at least four weeks notice in writing to end the tenancy;

LANDLORD'S OBLIGATIONS

The landlord agrees:

(a)   not to interrupt or interfere with the tenant's right to peacefully occupy the premises;

(b)   to keep in good repair, the structure and exterior of the premises including

        (i)   drains, gutters and external pipes;

        (ii)   the roof;

        (iii)   outside walls, outside doors, window sills, window catches, window frames;

        (iv)   internal walls, floors and ceilings, doors and door frames, door hinges and skirting boards;

        (v)   chimneys, chimney stacks and flues but not including sweeping;

        (vi)   pathways, steps or other means of access;

        (vii) plaster work;

        (viii) garages and doors;

        (ix)   boundary walls

(c)   to keep in good repair and working order any installations provided by the landlord for space heating and sanitation and for the supply of water, gas and electricity including:

        (i)   basins, sinks, baths, toilets, flushing systems and water pipes;

        (ii)   electrical wiring including sockets and switches, gas pipes and water pipes;

        (iii)   water heaters, fireplaces, fitted fires and central heating installations.

GENERAL

[ ]   The premises are to be let unfurnished.

[ ]   The premises are let partly/fully furnished and attached is an inventory of all the furniture and furnishings provided for the tenants use.

DECLARATION

Tenant:

I _____ hereby confirm that I understand and accept the terms of the agreement.

Signed: _____

Signature of witness: _____

Print name: _____

Date: _____

Landlord:

Signed: _____

Signature of witness: _____

Print name: _____

Date: _____

NOTICE REQUIRING POSSESSION OF A PROPERTY IN ENGLAND LET ON AN ASSURED SHORTHOLD TENANCY

FORM NO. 6A

Housing Act 1988 section 21(1) and (4) (as amended)

INFORMATION FOR THE TENANT

This notice tells you that your landlord requires possession of your home.
You should read it carefully and seek advice about your circumstances as quickly as possible.

You are entitled to at least two months' notice before being required to give up possession of your home. In some circumstances a longer notice period may be required.

If you do not leave your home by the date given in section 2, your landlord may apply to the court for an order under Section 21(1) or (4) of the Housing Act 1988 requiring you to give up possession.

If you are worried about this notice, and what you should do about it, take it immediately to Citizens Advice, a housing advice centre, a law centre or a solicitor.

If you are a debtor and you are in a 'breathing space', you should inform your debt advisor.

If you believe you are at risk of homelessness as a result of receiving this notice, you should contact your local authority for support.

Free independent advice is also available from Shelterline on 0808 800 4444 or via the Shelter website at: https://www.shelter.org.uk/.

Further information about this notice and the possession process can be found at: https://www.gov.uk/government/publications/understanding-the-possession-action-process-guidance-for-landlords-and-tenants

1. To: *(insert full name(s) of tenant(s))*

   Mr Donald Trump

2. You are required to leave the below address after: *(insert calendar date)*

   1 December 2023

   If you do not leave, your landlord may apply to the court for an order under Section 21(1) or (4) of the Housing Act 1988 requiring you to give up possession of: *(insert address of the property)*

   ....
   1 The White House, UPTON, UP1 2RG.
   ....

Page 1 of 2

Landlord and Tenant

3. If your landlord does not apply to the court within a given timeframe this notice will lapse. If you are entitled to more than 2 months', notice your landlord can rely on this notice to apply to the court during the period of 4 months commencing from the date specified in section 2 above. In all other cases, your landlord can rely on this notice to apply to the court during the period of 6 months commencing from the date this notice is given to you.

4. Name and address of landlord or landlord's agent:
(To be completed in full by the landlord, or, in the case of joint landlords, at least one of the joint landlords, or by someone authorised to give notice on the landlord's behalf.)

Signed ······ J Kennedy ···

Name ······ JOHN KENNEDY ···

Address ······ Lakeside Drive, Dallas Road, UPTON, UP2 3TR ···

Telephone number ······ 01245 67890 ···

Signed ···

Name ··

Address ···

Telephone number ···

Capacity *(please tick):*   landlord

~~joint landlord(s)~~

~~landlord's agent~~

Date ······ 20 September 2023 ···

113

Extracts from Claim Form N5b:

Claim form for possession of a property located in England

(Accelerated procedure)
(Assured shorthold tenancy other than a demoted tenancy)

Is the property you are claiming possession of located wholly or partly in England?

SEAL

☐ Yes

☐ No, the property is located wholly in Wales, use form **N5B WALES**.

Enter the full name(s) of the Claimant(s)

Enter the full name(s) of the Defendant(s)

The Claimant is claiming possession of

for the reasons given in the following pages

Important – to the Defendant(s)

This claim means that the Court will decide whether or not you have to leave the property and, if so, when. **There will not normally be a hearing. You must act immediately.**

Get help and advice from an advice agency or a solicitor.

Read all the pages of this form and the papers delivered with it.

Fill in the defence form (N11B England) and send or deliver it to the court named above.

You must send or deliver the defence form so that it arrives at court by [   ].

If you fail to do so, the Court may make a possession order against you.

Name and address of the court

Claim no.

Issue date

Fee Account no. (if applicable)

Help with Fees Ref no. (if applicable)

HWF

Court fee

Legal representative's costs

Total amount

6. On what date was the property let to the Defendant by way of a written tenancy agreement?

Day   Month   Year

The tenancy did not immediately follow an assured tenancy which was not an assured shorthold tenancy.

7. The tenancy agreement is dated

Day   Month   Year

A copy of the tenancy agreement is attached marked 'A'.

8. Has any subsequent written tenancy agreement been entered into?

☐ Yes
☐ No

If Yes -

The Defendant has been granted

☐ a further tenancy
☐ further tenancies

of the property by way of written agreement(s).

☐ This tenancy was
☐ These tenancies were

granted on the dates listed in the box below

A copy of each such tenancy agreement is attached and marked 'A1', 'A2' etc.

9a. Was the first tenancy and any agreement for it made on or after 28 February 1997?

☐ Yes, **answer questions 9b to 9g**

☐ No

9b. Was a notice served on the Defendant stating that any tenancy would not be, or would cease to be, an assured shorthold tenancy?

☐ Yes

☐ No

9c. Is there any provision in any tenancy agreement which states that it is not an assured shorthold tenancy?

☐ Yes

☐ No

9d. Is the 'agricultural worker condition' defined in Schedule 3 to the Housing Act 1988 fulfilled with respect to the property?

☐ Yes

☐ No

9e. Did any tenancy arise by way of succession under s.39 of the Housing Act 1988?

☐ Yes

☐ No

9f. Was any tenancy previously a secure tenancy under s.79 of the Housing Act 1985?

☐ Yes

☐ No

9g. Did any tenancy arise under Schedule 10 to the Local Government and Housing Act 1989 (at the end of a long residential tenancy)?

☐ Yes

☐ No

10. A notice in writing (under s.21 of the Housing Act 1988), saying that possession of the property was required, was served upon the Defendant(s).

10a. How was the notice served?

10b. On what date was the notice served?

Day   Month   Year

10c. Who served the notice?

10d. Who was the notice served on?

10e. After what date did the notice require the Defendant to leave the property?

Day   Month   Year

You must attach a copy of that notice and mark it 'B'. You can also include any proof of service marked 'B1'.

11a. Is the property required to be licensed under Part 2 (Houses in Multiple Occupation) or Part 3 (Selective Licensing) of the Housing Act 2004?

☐ Yes

     Is there a valid licence?

       ☐ Yes

       ☐ No

You must attach a copy of the licence and mark it 'C'.

☐ No

11b. Is a decision outstanding as to licensing, or as to a temporary exemption notice?

☐ Yes

You must attach evidence of the relevant application, notification, or appeal and mark it 'D'.

☐ No

12. Was a deposit paid in connection with the current tenancy or any prior tenancy of the property to which the Defendant was a party?

☐ Yes

☐ No

13. Has the deposit been returned to the Defendant (or the person – if not the Defendant – who paid the deposit)?

☐ Yes, the deposit was returned on

Day	Month	Year

☐ No

14. If the answer to question 12 is YES, and the deposit has not been returned, a copy of the Tenancy Deposit Scheme Certificate must be attached, marked 'E', and the following questions must be answered:

14a. Has the Claimant given to the Defendant, and to anyone who paid the deposit on behalf of the Defendant, the prescribed information?

☐ Yes

☐ No

14b. On what date was the prescribed information given?

Day	Month	Year

You must attach a copy of the Tenancy Deposit Scheme Certificate and mark it 'E'.

Page 9

118

15. Has the Claimant been served with a relevant notice in relation to the condition of the property or relevant common parts under s.11, s.12 or s.40(7) of the Housing Act 2004?

☐ Yes, **answer 15a to 15k**

☐ No, **go to question 16**

If Yes –

15a. On what date was the notice served?

Day	Month	Year

15b. Has the operation of the relevant notice been suspended?

☐ Yes

☐ No

If you have answered 'Yes'

(i) has the period of suspension ended?

☐ Yes

☐ No

(ii) on what date did the suspension end?

Day	Month	Year

15c. Has the relevant notice been revoked under s.16 of the Housing Act 2004?

☐ Yes

☐ No

15d. Has the relevant notice been quashed under paragraph 15 of Schedule 1 of the Housing Act 2004?

☐ Yes

☐ No

15e. Has a decision of the local housing authority not to revoke the relevant notice been reversed under paragraph 18 of Schedule 1 of the Housing Act 2004?

☐ Yes

☐ No

15f. Has a decision of the housing authority to take the action to which the relevant notice relates been reversed under section 45 of the Housing Act 2004?

☐ Yes

☐ No

15g. Did the Defendant complain or try to complain about the relevant condition of the property or the common parts to the Claimant before the notice was given?

☐ Yes

☐ No

15h. Is the relevant condition of the property or common parts due to a breach of duty or contract on the part of the Defendant?

☐ Yes

☐ No

15i. Is the property genuinely on the market for sale with intent to sell to an independent person not associated with the Claimant?

☐ Yes

☐ No

15j. Is the Claimant a private registered provider of social housing?

☐ Yes

☐ No

15k. Is the Claimant a mortgagee whose mortgage predated the tenancy and who requires vacant possession to sell the property under an existing power of sale?

☐ Yes

☐ No

16. Was a valid energy performance certificate given, free of charge, to the Defendant?

☐ Yes, the Defendant was given the certificate on

Day	Month	Year

You must attach a copy of the energy performance certificate and mark it 'F'.

☐ No

17. Is there any relevant gas fitting (including any gas appliance or installation pipework) installed in or serving the property?

☐ Yes, **answer question 17a, 17b and 17c**

☐ No, **go to question 18**

17a. Was a copy of a valid gas safety record provided to the Defendant before they went into occupation of the property?

☐ Yes

☐ No

Chapter 7

CONSUMER DISPUTES AND DEBT MATTERS

It is becoming more difficult for the lay person to obtain the services of a legal professional to take on a consumer dispute from beginning to end. The reason is that many consumer disputes involve amounts of money that in legal terms are small claims. Although the amounts of money involved are often small, these types of disputes frequently produce interesting and complicated points of law. This chapter will focus on a few selected areas: disputes involving the Consumer Credit Act and associated legislation and the Consumer Rights Act 2015.

Beware the source of help

Consumer disputes are the type of issues that frequent online forums. This may be because the majority of disputes are small in value although not of little importance to those involved. The small sums involved do not make it economical to pay lawyers to take on the whole case. There are bodies such as Which, that from time to time will take on a test case that may have important implications for a large number of people. As it may not be economical to have legal representation, many self-appointed "experts" appear on the internet offering advice. Some of it can be useful in giving some general information and useful pointers but you should be aware of that old saying, "a little knowledge is a dangerous thing". These sites may be useful but the advantage of the professional and practicing lawyer is that they not only have the knowledge of the law but they have the practical experience of being able to apply the law to the facts of a particular case. As in many professions, having had the experience at the sharp end is often worth a lot more than simply possessing the theoretical knowledge. In the legal sphere, this equates to knowing what a court in reality would decide in a particular situation. This is often learnt by the lawyer having gone through the painful experience of having tried what they thought was a brilliant argument out of a legal problem, only to appear in court to have that argument shot down in seconds. Such experiences teach you the art of the possible.

Legal telephone help lines have their uses but they can also be a victim of their own limitations, in that they could raise expectations because all a help line adviser can do is to give you the general legal position without really having the time to examine the particular circumstances. That is fine if the case is clear cut either way. The help line will usually play safe by saying, "it might be 'x' or it could be 'y'," without actually giving an opinion. One can understand the reason for this sitting on the fence because of a fear of complaints and some sanction by one of the many Ombudsmen that have developed in recent years. The growth in the number of Ombudsmen would seem to reflect the layperson's desire to complain and the fact that we are encouraged to complain. If this continues we will have an Ombudsman for everything from a Legal Ombudsman to an Ombudsman for dog walkers!

What you may ask has this ramble got to do with consumer law and representing yourself in court? Well, the point that is relevant is that consumer law produces a lot of litigants in person and if you are contemplating taking a case through court you should stand back and consider objectively whether your complaint is simply an overreaction and does it have any basis in law? There are many things in life that are irritating but not all irritations make the basis of a law suit. There is a climate which has emerged, which might have migrated from the United States, that the customer is always right. This attitude that the customer is always right does not make the basis of a legal action. Probably because the County Court has in recent years been swamped with small consumer claims, there has been a push to make parties use alternative dispute resolution such as mediation and ombudsmen schemes. Ombudsmen schemes have their uses and are particularly suited to considering levels of service but their remit is not the same as a court as they consider what is "fair and reasonable" as opposed to what is the law. Often what is fair and reasonable will match what the law is but not always.

Consumer Credit Act cases

It important to note that this section is not intended to be a comprehensive statement of the law relating to consumer credit. Consumer credit is a very complex area with many pieces of legislation that need to be fully understood. The purpose behind this section is to examine some of the common themes that arise in consumer cases and to give guidance on how the litigant in person can prepare a case where they may have grounds for defending a claim. So, for example, it will give you some of the basic information to consider and may lead the litigant to get further and more expert advice on a particular aspect.

Consumer credit in the UK is regulated by the Consumer Credit Act 1974 (amended in 2006), the Financial Services and Markets Act 2000 and various regulations implementing European Union consumer credit law. The legislation covers the following areas:

- the information consumers should be provided with before they enter into a credit agreement
- the content and form of credit agreements
- the method of calculating annual percentage rates of interest (APR)
- procedures relating to events of default, termination and early settlement
- credit advertising
- additional protection for credit card purchases costing more than £100 and up to £30,000 under Section 75 of the Consumer Credit Act

- the requirements as to the production of statements (Section 6 of the Consumer Credit Act 2006 inserted a new section (s77A) whereby a statement must be provided if the agreement is a fixed sum credit agreement under section 77A.)

When the financial crisis happened in 2008, there were many borrowers/credit card holders who faced being in default and the lenders took action to terminate the agreements and recover the sums due. When faced with thousands of pounds of debt, it is understandable that the debtor will consider whether there are any legal issues which will enable them to escape liability and probable bankruptcy. Some may say that as they took out the loan and had the money then they should pay it back and not try to find some obscure provision to avoid paying their debts. Such behaviour in their opinion is morally reprehensible. On the other hand, the organisations who lend the money and provide the credit cards should know the legal requirements or have the resources to check the rules and so there is no excuse if they do not comply with the law. Those who lend money are required to have a consumer credit licence and to obtain such a licence they have to display that they are aware of the legal requirements. If they follow the correct procedures, then very few borrowers would be able to avoid payment.

A typical example of a process which can lead to borrowers being able to exploit the legal process is where, for example, a credit card company sells off many accounts to a credit purchaser a number of years after the accounts have gone into default. The debt purchaser will probably pay a few pence in the pound for each debt and therefore anything it manages to recover from the debtor is a reasonable return. The original creditor also believes that it is better to sell the accounts for a much-reduced price than to spend the time and effort in recovering the monies due. But, herein lies the problem, and hence the ability of the tenacious borrower to escape payment of the loan. It may seem unjust but if Consumer Credit legislation was introduced to protect consumers from unfair practices, is it unfair for the consumer to utilise the legislation if the lender has made a mistake? It might be said that the law is weighted too heavily in favour of the consumer in that if the consumer makes a mistake, they are not faced with the same dire consequences, e.g., not being able to enforce payment of a loan, as those faced by the creditor.

The following example of **Big Credit Card Company v. Joe Balance** is a typical consumer case that may arise under consumer credit legislation:

Big Credit Card Company v. Joe Balance

> *On 10 January xxxx, Joe Balance signed up for a credit card with the Big Credit Card Company Ltd ("BCCC"). Joe Balance had a credit limit of £3,000 on the card. Things were fine for the first year as Joe paid off the balance each month in full. In early xxxx, Joe lost his job because of a downturn in the industry he worked in. This caused him to miss payments on the credit card and by September xxxx, BCCC served a notice of default on Joe and terminated the agreement in December xxxx. The amount due on termination was £10,200. Joe received chasing letters from BCCC. In July xxxx, he received a Court Claim with We Purchase Any Debt Ltd ("WPAD") named as the Claimant. The Claim Form is set out at the end of this chapter.*

The starting point with these types of cases is to look at the Credit Agreement and to see if it complies with the requirements of the Consumer Credit Act 1974 (as amended by the 2006 Act) and associated Regulations. The Consumer Credit Act sets out certain requirements that a regulated agreement must contain. Therefore, you should begin by looking at the agreement you signed.

Is it a regulated agreement?

A regulated consumer credit agreement is defined as an agreement between two parties, one of whom (the debtor) is an individual, and the other of whom (the creditor) is "any other person", in which the creditor provides the debtor with credit not exceeding £5,000 (this figure was subsequently increased to £25,000 and under the Consumer Credit Act 2006 there is no upper limit).

What must the agreement contain?

The credit agreement must contain the following specific information in writing for it to be legally binding and enforceable by law:

- Length of the agreement
- Amount you are borrowing
- Amount and frequency of payments
- Type of agreement, such as credit sale or hire purchase
- Total charge for credit and the annual percentage rate of interest (APR)
- Details of your cancellation rights (if applicable) and other forms of protection and remedies available

If the credit agreement does not contain all of this information, the lender might not be able to enforce the agreement without first getting the court's permission.

If the agreement does not contain something that it should under the legislation or there seems to have been an error in the execution of the agreement, then whether or not that will make the agreement permanently unenforceable will depend on when the agreement was signed. Different rules apply to agreements signed before 6 April 2007. Agreements executed before 6 April 2007 are subject to sections 127 (3) & (4) of the Consumer Credit Act 1974 ('CCA'). These sections do not apply to Agreements entered into after 6 April 2007 by operation of the repeal under the Consumer Credit Act 2006.

Before 6 April 2007, section 127 of Consumer Credit Act was as follows:

127 Enforcement orders in cases of infringement

(1) In the case of an application for an enforcement order under—
(a)section 65(1) (improperly executed agreements), or
(b)section 105(7)(a) or (b) (improperly executed security instruments), or
(c)section 111(2) (failure to serve copy of notice on surety),

or
(d)section 124(1) or (2) (taking of negotiable instrument in contravention of section 123),

the court shall dismiss the application if, but (subject to subsections (3) and (4)) only if, it considers it just to do so having regard to—

(i)prejudice caused to any person by the contravention in question, and the degree of culpability for it; and
(ii)the powers conferred on the court by subsection (2) and sections 135 and 136.

(2) If it appears to the court just to do so, it may in an enforcement order reduce or discharge any sum payable by the debtor or hirer, or any surety, so as to compensate him for prejudice suffered as a result of the contravention in question.

(3) The court shall not make an enforcement order under section 65(1) if section 61(1)(a) (signing of agreements) was not complied with unless a document (whether or not in the prescribed form and complying with regulations under section 60(1)) itself containing all the prescribed terms of the agreement was signed by the debtor or hirer (whether or not in the prescribed manner).

(4) The court shall not make an enforcement order under section 65(1) in the case of a cancellable agreement if—
(a) a provision of section 62 or 63 was not complied with, and the creditor or owner did not give a copy of the executed agreement, and of any other document referred to in it, to the debtor or hirer before the commencement of the proceedings in which the order is sought, or

(b)section 64(1) was not complied with.

(5) Where an enforcement order is made in a case to which subsection (3) applies, the order may direct that the regulated agreement is to have effect as if it did not include a term omitted from the document signed by the debtor or hirer.

After 6 April 2007, section 127 (3), (4) and (5) were repealed by the Consumer Credit Act 2006 and section 127 is now as follows:

127 Enforcement orders in cases of infringement.

(1) In the case of an application for an enforcement order under—

(za) section 55(2) (disclosure of information), or

(zb) section 61B(3) (duty to supply copy of overdraft agreement), or

(a) section 65(1) (improperly executed agreements), or

(b) section 105(7)(a) or (b) (improperly executed security instruments), or

(c) section 111(2) (failure to serve copy of notice on surety), or

(d) section 124(1) or (2) (taking of negotiable instrument in contravention of section 123),

the court shall dismiss the application if, but only if, it considers it just to do so having regard to—

(i) prejudice caused to any person by the contravention in question, and the degree of culpability for it; and

(ii) the powers conferred on the court by subsection (2) and sections 135 and 136.

(2) If it appears to the court just to do so, it may in an enforcement order reduce or discharge any sum payable by the debtor or hirer, or any surety, so as to compensate him for prejudice suffered as a result of the contravention in question.

What this means in practice is that, for agreements entered into after 6 April 2007, if the Agreement was not properly executed then it will only be enforceable by an Order of the Court. So the creditor would ask the court to exercise its discretion and make an enforcement order; under section 127 (2) the judge can decide whether to permit enforcement or could reduce the sum payable or even discharge it totally depending on how the judge views the extent of the contravention by the creditor and the level of prejudice to the debtor.

To see whether there were defects in the credit agreement requires finding your agreement which many people may have long since lost. There was a spate of cases that attempted to get debtors out of paying the sum demanded because people felt that section 78 of the Consumer Credit Act 1974 provided them with a Defence. The case of **Carey v. HSBC (2009)** made it very clear that the creditor needs to provide a true copy of the executed agreement, and where the original had been varied either a copy of each discrete term that had been varied or a copy of the current terms and conditions as the contract stands at the date of the request. The creditor does not need to send a photocopy of the original agreement although many people still think (wrongly) that they do. The High Court in the case of Carey ruled that the underlying purpose of section 78 is for information you need about the terms of your contract. The creditor has a duty to ensure the copy is "honest and accurate". It can be a reconstituted agreement; by this it is meant that the creditor can type up the terms or it can use a template which was in use at the time you took out your agreement and then enter your information. The burden rests on the debtor to say why it is not accurate. So a photocopy of the original isn't needed, but what is needed is that the creditor must produce in an easily legible format the terms of your contract.

In the case of Big Credit Card Company and Joe Balance, there were no defects in the agreement itself and so we should consider other aspects. The Particulars of Claim are rather brief and vague; there are a few questions and disclosures which will show whether this claim is likely to succeed. The Claim states that the Agreement was Assigned to We Buy Any Debt Ltd. Joe should ask for a copy of the Assignment. He claims not to have seen a copy of the Notice of Assignment. The Claimant is going to have to show that he has standing to bring the Claim, ie that he actually bought the debt. If We Buy Any Debt Ltd do not own the debt they are not entitled to bring the Claim. It is not uncommon for a debt purchaser to refuse to provide a copy of the Assignment on the basis that it contains confidential information and that they are not permitted to produce it on grounds of Data Protection. This is an attempt to dodge the issue as there are exemptions under the Data Protection Act 2018 which permits disclosure for the purposes of, or in connection with:

- legal proceedings, including prospective legal proceedings;
- obtaining legal advice; or
- establishing, exercising or defending legal rights.

If faced with such an excuse the reply should be that without production, they cannot prove the entitlement to bring the claim. So they might say that they cannot provide the information because of data protection but this section provides an exemption where disclosure is required to exercise or defend legal rights. It is possible they will still refuse but then an application for disclosure could be made to the court and the court would most likely Order the Assignment to be disclosed. You could take the view that if they are reluctant to disclose it then perhaps they do not have the document which would ultimately cause them a problem if they proceed to a trial because We Buy Any Debt Ltd would have difficulty proving that they have standing to bring the claim. They could obtain a witness statement saying the debt was assigned but they are going to need someone with direct knowledge of the signed document and it is unlikely that person would come to the trial. Therefore, without a copy of the document, they would probably not be able to prove on the balance of probability that they purchased the debt.

If the case progresses to a trial one of the stages of the claim will be "disclosure". The assignment would be a document that We Buy Any Debt should have to disclose. If they do not disclose it to Joe Balance then he could make an application for specific disclosure. (We shall return to the issue of disclosure of the Assignment later in this chapter).

A debtor is entitled to see a copy of the Assignment and this was made clear in the case of **Van Lynn Developments Limited v. Pelias Construction Company Limited (formerly Jason Construction Company Limited) (1968)**. Lord Denning said in his judgment *"After receiving the notice, the debtor will be entitled, of course, to require a sight of the assignment so as to be satisfied that it is valid, and that the assigns can give him a good discharge."*

The issues and questions about an assignment often arise where debt purchase companies buy debts. The debts are bought for a few pence from Credit Card and Loan companies in the hope that they can recover something for little effort, apart from some chasing by debt collectors or the threat (and possibly issue) of court proceedings. Companies that sell the debt do not want to get involved in any disputes after the sale and this creates a problem for the debt purchaser. They probably have limited documentation and if a matter does progress to a court hearing they struggle to prove their case.

The case of **PRA v. Brunt (4 Feb 2015)** provides a good example of a debt purchaser struggling to establish that the debt was assigned. It was heard by Her Honour Judge Melissa Clarke in Reading County Court. There was a preliminary issue as to whether PRA as the current claimant had the right to pursue the debt. The claimant's case was that the debt arose under an agreement and MBNA was the original creditor. MBNA assigned the debt to Vardy Investments (Ireland) Ltd ("Vardy"), pursuant to an agreement dated 31st July 2009. Vardy assigned the debt to Aktiv pursuant to an agreement dated 29th February 2012 (the original claimant in the proceedings), and Aktiv assigned the debt to PRA in December 2014. The judge had very limited information. The agreement between Aktiv and Vardy that had been filed as evidence by the claimant is extremely heavily redacted. The redactions were so heavy that they include a redaction of any evidence as to execution of the document. It was impossible to tell whether this document had been executed at all and there was no specific evidence elsewhere that the agreement had in fact been properly executed. The judge said it looked like, *"something released under the 30-year rule by one of the security services"*. There was no specific evidence provided by anybody who was in a position to know, or by any specific documentation, that Mr Brunt's name was on a list of debts assigned by Vardy to Aktiv. Therefore, the judge dismissed the claim.

The reality is that if a debtor asks a few legitimate questions it is going to be very difficult for the debt purchaser to prove on the balance of probability that the debt was assigned, especially if the debt purchaser is not prepared to release a copy of the assignment without it being heavily redacted. It is unlikely to have a witness who can give direct evidence on the assignment because often this will have taken place some years before and so are very unlikely to come to court. I do not know why in so many of these cases there is a reluctance to reveal the assignment. One would have thought that if there was nothing wrong with the document then its disclosure would close down this argument and, providing the other aspects of their paperwork were in order, they would be home and dry. There might be something in the nature of these assignments between credit card companies and debt purchasers which they do not want revealed or the debt purchaser cannot release the document as they are bound by a confidentiality clause and believe that risking a breach of that is a greater risk than losing a few court cases which are often within the small claims limit of £10,000 and so the costs consequences are not substantial. It might be that when you examine the assignment document, there is something in it that actually confirms that it was an equitable assignment because the assignment was not absolute, which means that the original creditor retains an interest such as the fact that the debt purchaser has to pay some of the money it recovers to the original creditor.

Whether the assignment was a "legal" assignment or an "equitable" assignment is an important point to consider. A legal assignment is one that complies with the requirements under section 136 of the Law of Property Act 1925 which states:

> *136 Legal assignments of things in action.*
>
> *(1) Any absolute assignment by writing under the hand of the assignor (not purporting to be by way of charge only) of any debt or other legal thing in action, of which express notice in writing has been given to the debtor, trustee or other person from whom the assignor would have been entitled to claim such debt or thing in action, is effectual in law (subject to equities having priority over the right of the assignee) to pass and transfer from the date of such notice—*
>
> *(a) the legal right to such debt or thing in action;*
>
> *(b) all legal and other remedies for the same; and*
>
> *(c) the power to give a good discharge for the same without the concurrence of the assignor:*
>
> *Provided that, if the debtor, trustee or other person liable in respect of such debt or thing in action has notice—*
>
> *(a) that the assignment is disputed by the assignor or any person claiming under him; or*
>
> *(b) of any other opposing or conflicting claims to such debt or thing in action; he may, if he thinks fit, either call upon the persons making claim thereto to interplead concerning the same, or pay the debt or other thing in action into court under the provisions of the Trustee Act, 1925.*

If the requirements of section 136 are not complied with it can still be an assignment but it will not be a "legal" assignment but instead an "equitable assignment". What this section in summary means is that for something to be a legal assignment that certain legal formalities must be complied with. These formalities are:

- An absolute assignment in writing signed by the assignor;
- A debt or other legal thing in action; and
- Express notice in writing to the debtor.

The significance in many cases as to whether it is a legal or an equitable assignment arises on the procedural aspects. A legal assignment within the Act transfers a legal right to the assignee. Consequently the assignee sues the debtor in his own name. If there is an equitable assignment and the assignment is absolute, then again the assignee is entitled to sue in his own name. However, if there is an equitable assignment, the assignor must be joined into the action either as claimant, if he co-operates, or as defendant if he does not. If the assignor is not joined as a party, the assignee's action may well fail although it is important to stress that these requirements are procedural and are not substantive, therefore the courts have the discretion to dispense with the need to have the assignor as a party.

If it was an equitable assignment and the court will not dispense with the need to join the original creditor, then that again causes problems for the debt purchaser because, as has been said, the original creditor will most likely not want to be involved. This might explain why in many cases, when the debtor stands firm on the issue of assignment, the debt purchaser withdraws the case.

We Purchase Any Debt Ltd v. Joseph Balance – The Defence

Having considered the likely issues involved in a Consumer Credit Act dispute, now let's turn to what Joe Balance might include in his defence

1. *The Defendant admits that it entered into a regulated consumer credit agreement 2 January xxxx. The Agreement was a "cancellable agreement" but the Agreement did not provide details of the Defendant's right to cancel the Agreement. Therefore, the Agreement is not enforceable without an order of the Court. The Defendant asks the court to make an Order under section 127 (2) of the Consumer Credit Act 1974 as amended, discharging any debt that may be payable.*

2. *The Claimant is put to strict proof that it has standing to bring this claim. The Defendant contends that he did not receive any Notice of Assignment relating to the Agreement. The Claimant is put to strict proof that Big Credit Card Company   Ltd assigned the balance due under the contract.*

The Defence is based on two issues:

- The credit agreement did not contain details of the right to cancel and therefore it is only enforceable if there is an Order from the Court. As we have seen, under section 127 of the Consumer Credit Act 1974 as amended, the court has discretion to reduce the amount payable or totally discharge the debt.
- The second part of the defence requires the Claimant to prove that they have standing to bring the claim which means that they will have to produce evidence to satisfy the court that the debt was assigned from Big Credit card Company to We Buy Any Debt.

Where a Claim was issued through the County Court Business Centre and a Defence is filed, the Claimant is required to contact the County Court Business Centre within 28 days to say whether they wish to proceed with the claim. Therefore, Joe Balance should receive a Notice as set out at the end of this Chapter. If We Buy Any Debt Ltd does not respond to the court within 28 days, then the claim will become stayed. It is likely that many of these cases will remain in this limbo for long periods of time while the

Claimant decides if they can locate the paperwork to have a real prospect of succeeding if it progressed the claim to trial. One does have to question the logic in issuing the claim before it is sure of the documentary evidence to support the debt. Of course it is possible that the debt purchasers who take these proceedings had an honest belief that they thought they would be able to locate the documents if the claim was defended and genuinely believed the facts they set out, but litigation is in a new legal world where the rules and requirements have changed. These new requirements work against the viability of large-scale debt recovery, especially of smaller claims because having all your information in order at the start may mean that the front loading of these costs to the pre-action stage affects the viability of pursuing these claims. The reality is that some debtors know that this is the case and will take advantage; some may well get away without paying a debt that is legitimately due.

What a litigant must remember though is that if they file a Defence, it contains a statement of truth which they have to sign. The Statement of Truth is where the party confirms that the facts in the document are true; signing a statement of truth knowing that the facts are false is a serious matter and contempt of court proceedings could follow. So, a litigant who thinks that it is okay to lie on a court document because they think the Claimant will not prove otherwise is wrong and faces serious consequences.

Making a settlement

Having looked at all the angles of a claim, such as the one brought by **We Purchase Any Debt Ltd v. Joseph Balance**, if there is no defence to the claim then you should consider whether the Claimant would consider a reduced offer in settlement of the debt or whether they would be prepared to accept payment in instalments. A debt purchaser who has probably only paid a fraction of the debt is likely to accept a reasonable offer.

Key points in a Consumer Credit Matter

- **Is it a regulated agreement?**
- **Did the agreement contain everything as required by the Legislation?**
- **If the agreement was assigned, has the Claimant shown that they have standing to bring the claim? Have they produced a copy of the assignment? Have they given notice of the assignment?**
- **If it was an equitable assignment, has the original creditor been joined into the proceedings?**
- **Has the creditor complied with their obligations to provide statements?**

Debt Actions and setting aside unknown County Court Judgments (CCJ's)

There is a growing problem with creditors/debt purchase companies issuing proceedings and applying for Judgments against a defendant at a previous or incorrect address of the Defendant. A typical scenario is that a person may be credit checked for a mortgage and discover that they are turned down because of a CCJ entered against them from a long time ago at an address they have not lived at for many years. There is some suspicion that little care is taken by some organisations to ensure that the court papers are correctly served. An individual or a business, faced with an old CCJ which is hampering their credit, will then worry as to what they can do to rectify the situation. The following section explains the grounds on which a county court judgment can be set aside and if there are grounds, the procedure, for doing so. It should made clear that the purpose of this section is not to condone deliberate "credit cleaning". It is simply to assist those in situations where they have genuine grounds to overturn a CCJ.

The following example is typical of a person discovering a CCJ registered against them at a previous address:

> *Sophie Smith and Brian Edwards, are in the process of buying a new house together. They have been in rented accommodation at 125 Swindon Gardens, Upton, for the last 12 months and they have now applied for a mortgage to buy their new home. The mortgage is turned down as they are told that Sophie has had a CCJ against her name from two years ago when Sophie lived on her own at another rented place, 34 Pond Street, Upton. Sophie makes enquiries as to who is the company that obtained the Judgment. Credit Card Debt Purchase Ltd (CCDP) is the Claimant who issued proceedings. The amount of the Judgment is £2,000. Sophie recalls that she had a credit card with Green Card Plc and three years ago she was being chased by them for a debt of £1,500 but she was disputing it on a number of grounds including defective execution of a Consumer Credit Agreement signed in xxxx. Sophie finds it rather strange that she did not receive any letters about this disputed credit card debt. She is told by CCDP that they bought the debt 6 months ago. Sophie says that not long after they moved in to 125 Swindon Gardens, she had a call from Green Card (as she has kept the same mobile number) and she argued that she contested the debt and gave them her new address on the telephone and said, "if you feel the CCA agreement is enforceable, then take me to court". CCDP say that the Judgment was correctly entered as the court proceedings were sent to her last known address and deny that she had given them her new address.*

The starting point is to consider where a Claim against an individual should be served under the court rules. Under CPR Part 6.9(2), where the Defendant is an individual, if no address for service is given then the Claim Form should be served at the "usual or last known residence". It is possible that service at the usual or last known residence can be effective service even though the defendant does not receive the claim form. To help prevent this unfairness from happening, CPR Part 6.9(3) provides that where a claimant has reason to believe that the Defendant may no longer reside at their usual or last known address, the claimant must take reasonable steps to ascertain the address of the defendant's current residence. If those reasonable enquiries cannot discover the defendant's current address, the claimant must consider whether the defendant could be served at an alternative place or by an alternative method and, if so, should make an application for alternative service. If all steps have failed to locate the defendant's address for service, the claimant believes the defendant no longer resides at the address specified in CPR Part 6.9(2) but reasonable enquiries have not revealed the defendant's current address and service by an alternative method is not possible, then the claimant may effect valid service on the defendant at the address in CPR Part 6.9 (2) [the usual or last known residence]. To non-lawyers, this is rather bizarre; the claimant can in these circumstances serve a claim form at an address he knows the defendant is not at

You don't have to be a genius to work out that this rule can be exploited by ruthless claimants. Although, in this situation, a defendant would have grounds to apply to set aside, with court fees increasing it costs more to make an application and add to that the hassle factor of going through the process, defendants may feel pressurised into agreeing to pay back a County Court Judgment even though it has not been entered correctly and there are genuine legal grounds for overturning it.

In the case of Sophie Smith and Credit Card Debt Purchase Ltd (CCDP), she gave them her current address and CCDP for whatever reason decided to service it at her previous address (34 Pond Street, Upton). In this case, the Claim Form has not been properly served.

A litigant in person faced with the situation of Sophie Smith, should swiftly make an application to set aside Judgment. Before making the application, you should write to the claimant and set out the basis on which you will be applying to set aside the Judgment. In this example, the grounds on which she can ask the court to set it aside are:

- The Court Claim was not served on the Defendant
- The Defendant has a reasonable prospect of successfully defending the Claim.

Having a "reasonable prospect of success" is part of the test to be considered when an application to set aside is made. The full wording of the test is contained in CPR Part 13:

> a) the defendant has a real prospect of successfully defending the claim; or
> (b) it appears to the court that there is some other good reason why -
> (i) the judgment should be set aside or varied; or
> (ii) the defendant should be allowed to defend the claim.

If a Court Claim has been served correctly in accordance with the rules, then the fact that a Claim Form was not received does not automatically mean a Judgment should be set aside. However, a judge can use discretion as to whether this would be some "other good reason" as to why the Judgment should be set aside. When considering an application to set aside, one of the factors the court must consider is whether the person seeking to set aside the judgment made an application to do so promptly. It is important to remember that, as soon as you become aware of a Judgment, you should make an application to set aside if you have grounds for doing so. The court might expect it to take a week or two to seek advice but if you delay longer than a month before making an application, then the chances of succeeding may be affected.

As this type of application is a common one experienced by litigants in person, it is worth setting out the application in full and detail what it should contain. The Application needs to be on Form N244. A detailed witness statement should accompany the application to set out the facts.

A witness statement in support of the Application by Sophie Smith might read as follows:

I, Sophie Smith, of 125 Swindon Gardens, Upton, will say as follows:

1. I am the Defendant in this action and I make this application in support of my application to set aside judgment.
2. On or about the xx/xx/xx, I was applying for a mortgage with my partner, Brian Edwards. The mortgage was turned down as a County Court Judgment showed up against my name. I obtained the details of the Judgment from the Court and I noticed that the Judgment had been entered against me some two years ago at my previous address.
3. I contacted the Claimant and asked them what this Judgment related to as I did not recognise the name. They said that they bought the debt from Green Card Plc. I recall that I had a credit card with Green Card and about three years ago I was being chased by them for a debt of £1,500. I was disputing it on a number of grounds including defective execution of a Consumer Credit Agreement signed in xxxx. I refer to exhibit 1 which contains copies of correspondence I had with Green Card. As can been from the correspondence, I stated that I believed that I had a genuine ground for disputing the debt because the credit agreement had not contained all the required terms and information as it should have done under the Consumer Credit Act. I had written this letter to them after seeking legal advice from a local solicitor.
4. I did not receive any letters about this disputed credit card debt and nor have I received any notice that the account had been assigned to CCDP. I am surprised that I did not receive any letters and that the Claim Form was sent to my old address, because after I had moved to 125 Swindon Gardens, I had a call from Green Card and I said I contested the debt and gave them my new address.

5. I ask that the Judgment be set aside and that I be allowed to enter a Defence. I am told by the solicitor from whom I sought advice before making this Application, that the Claim by CCDP was not served in accordance with the civil procedure rules. In addition, I have a real prospect of successfully defending this claim as I have genuine reasons why the alleged debt on the credit card is not enforceable.

STATEMENT OF TRUTH

I believe that the facts stated in this witness statement are true. I understand that proceedings for contempt of court may be brought against anyone who makes, or causes to be made, a false statement in a document verified by a statement of truth without an honest belief in its truth.

Signed: *Sophie Smith*

Claim Form

In the	
COUNTY COURT BUSINESS CENTRE	
Claim No.	CBC23LK900
Issue Date	15 July 2023

Court Address

1688

COUNTY COURT BUSINESS CENTRE
4TH FLOOR ST KATHARINE'S HOUSE
21-27 ST KATHARINE'S STREET
NORTHAMPTON
NN1 2LH

Court telephone number:
0300 123 1056

Claimant

We Buy Any Debt Ltd
111 Bedford Row
LONDON
WCR 3BY

Address for sending documents and payments (if different)

Debt Recoveries Are Us Solicitors
Trinity Street
Upton
UP1 2HY

Ref: AR/345678

Mr Joseph Balance
23 Market Close
Upton
UP2 3PR

Defendant

Particulars of Claim

The Claimant claims payment of the
overdue balance due from the Defendant
under a contract between the Defendant
and Big Credit Card Company Ltd dated on
or around 11 January XXXX and assigned to
the Claimant on 30 November XXXX.
The Claimant claims £10,200 plus interest
according to section 69 of the County
Courts Act 1984.

Defendant

Important Note

* You have a limited time in which to reply to this
  claim form

* Please read all the guidance notes on the back of this
  form - they set out the time limits and tell you what
  you can do about the claim

* You can respond to this claim online. Log on to
  www.moneyclaim.gov.uk

* You will need the claim number (see above) and the
  following password j85xh93g

	£
Amount claimed	10,200.00
Court fee	459.00
Legal representative's costs	100.00
Total amount	10,759.00

The Claimant believes that the facts stated in this claim form
are true and I am duly authorised by the claimant to sign this
statement

Signed F G Marshall

N244

Application notice

For help in completing this form please read the notes for guidance form N244Notes.

Find out how HM Courts and Tribunals Service uses personal information you give them when you fill in a form: https://www.gov.uk/government/organisations/hm-courts-and-tribunals-service/about/personal-information-charter

Name of court		Claim no.
CCMCC		
Fee account no. (if applicable)		Help with Fees – Ref. no. (if applicable)
		H W F - ☐☐☐ - ☐☐☐
Warrant no. (if applicable)		
Claimant's name (including ref.) Credit Card Debt Purchase Ltd		
Defendant's name (including ref.) Sophie Smith		
Date		xx/xx/xx

1. What is your name or, if you are a legal representative, the name of your firm?

   Sophie Smith

2. Are you a   ☐ Claimant   ☑ Defendant   ☐ Legal Representative

   ☐ Other (please specify)

   If you are a legal representative whom do you represent?

3. What order are you asking the court to make and why?

   I am seeking an order to set aside Judgment because the Claim was not served in accordance with the Civil Procedure Rules and I have a real prospect of successfully defending the Claim.

4. Have you attached a draft of the order you are applying for?   ☑ Yes   ☐ No

5. How do you want to have this application dealt with?   ☑ at a hearing   ☐ without a hearing

   ☐ at a remote hearing

6. How long do you think the hearing will last?   [ ] Hours   [20] Minutes

   Is this time estimate agreed by all parties?   ☐ Yes   ☐ No

7. Give details of any fixed trial date or period   None

8. What level of Judge does your hearing need?   District Judge

9. Who should be served with this application?   Claimant

9a. Please give the service address, (other than details of the claimant or defendant) of any party named in question 9.

10. What information will you be relying on, in support of your application?

- ☑ the attached witness statement
- ☐ the statement of case
- ☐ the evidence set out in the box below

If necessary, please continue on a separate sheet.

2

11. Do you believe you, or a witness who will give evidence on your behalf, are vulnerable in any way which the court needs to consider?

☑ Yes. Please explain in what way you or the witness are vulnerable and what steps, support or adjustments you wish the court and the judge to consider.

☑ No

3

148

Statement of Truth

I understand that proceedings for contempt of court may be brought against a person who makes, or causes to be made, a false statement in a document verified by a statement of truth without an honest belief in its truth.

☑ **I believe** that the facts stated in section 10 (and any continuation sheets) are true.

☐ **The applicant believes** that the facts stated in section 10 (and any continuation sheets) are true. **I am authorised** by the applicant to sign this statement.

Signature

Sophie Smith

☑ Applicant

☐ Litigation friend (where applicant is a child or a Protected Party)

☐ Applicant's legal representative (as defined by CPR 2.3(1))

Date

Day	Month	Year
xx	xx	xx

Full name

Sophie Smith

Name of applicant's legal representative's firm

If signing on behalf of firm or company give position or office held

4

Applicant's address to which documents should be sent.

Building and street

125 Swim Gardens

Second line of address

Town or city

Upton

County (optional)

Postcode

U P 1 5 P A

If applicable

Phone number

01334 567 890

Fax phone number

DX number

Your Ref.

Email

sophiesmith@inbox.com

Chapter 8

BOUNDARY AND RIGHTS OF WAY DISPUTES

How does the law establish the position of a boundary?

Trying to establish the position of a boundary is not always an easy exercise. What many people do not realise is that the plans registered at the Land Registry only show the general position of the boundaries unless (which is unusual) the boundary has been specifically determined. In which case, that will be stated on the Title.

It is well known that boundary disputes create a lot of tension between neighbours (and generate a lot of legal fees), but still landowners continue to get drawn into what in many cases are futile arguments over a few inches of land. When you read further on you will discover how difficult it is to determine the exact boundaries and that should make you consider that going to court should really be the very last resort unless the matter is of significant importance. Often, the importance which a litigant places on a boundary is greater than it actually is when viewed objectively, but that is probably because the fuel that drives a boundary dispute is not always about the land on the ground but is associated with some underlying conflict between the neighbours.

Boundaries are created when an owner of a piece of land divides that land into smaller pieces, or parcels of land, and offers the small parcels for sale. It is the seller who describes (defines) the boundary. Boundaries are described in the earliest conveyance or transfer deed that describes the parcel of land in question. The definition may be expressed as words in the parcels clause of the deed, in a plan or a combination of both.

The basic principles to follow when it comes to establishing a disputed boundary were set out by Lord Hoffman in the House of Lords case of **Alan Wibberley Building Ltd v. Insley [1999] UKHL 15.**

- The first task is to review the title deeds.

- The parcels clause of a conveyance or transfer may refer to an attached plan, but usually this is said to be "for the purposes of identification only". The use of such words indicates that the plan cannot be relied upon as delineating the precise boundaries.

- It follows that, if someone has to establish an exact boundary, a conveyance or transfer will almost invariably have to be supplemented by inferences drawn from topographical features that existed (or may be supposed to have existed) at the time that the deed was executed, or from other evidence.

As has been pointed out, the Land Registry Title Plan only shows general boundaries and not the precise ones unless it is stated on the Title that the boundary has been "determined". As Lord Hoffman confirmed, the starting point is to look at the pre-registration title deeds which should generally be the primary source for establishing the boundary line. However, often deeds are not kept and so there is nothing to examine. If deeds are located then if there is a clear definition of the boundary and there is no ambiguity then extrinsic evidence will not be considered. Often though a description can be ambiguous and there may be a problem with the plan. If the deeds are not held or they cannot be located, there is a variety of extrinsic evidence that can be considered including:

- Particulars of sale at an auction or estate agent's particulars.
- Replies to pre-contract enquiries.
- Statutory declarations.

- Maps, including OS maps.
- Photographs - historic and new photographs are invaluable where plans are non-existent or so distorted it is almost impossible to decipher.
- Planning permissions.
- Decisions from earlier boundary dispute proceedings of neighbouring properties.

It is not always clear from some of the legal decisions as to when the evidence of the parties can be admissible. In the case of **Pennock v. Hodgson (2010)** the Court of Appeal stated that the subjective beliefs about the position of a disputed boundary is inadmissible. However, in the Court of Appeal case of **Ali v. Lane (2006)**, the court held that in the context of the conveyance of land where the information contained in the conveyance is unclear or ambiguous, it is permissible to have regard to the evidence of subsequent conduct, subject always to that evidence being of probative value in determining what the parties intended. What this means is that the evidence of subsequent conduct must be related to the state of affairs at the time of the original conveyance of land and the intentions of the original parties to the conveyance. This principle was applied in **Piper v. Wakefield (2008)** where a party to a conveyance later planted pine trees on the line of the boundary. The Court of Appeal accepted this as probative evidence of where the boundary of the original conveyance was intended to be.

What the above shows is that admissibility of extrinsic evidence can be a complicated question of law and is not something which a lay litigant in person would be expected to grasp; it is certainly an issue for a specialist lawyer in this field. This book does not intend therefore to go in great detail on this point except to say that where a conveyance is unclear a court will take into account external evidence as part of the surrounding circumstances and these will help indicate to a reasonable person the position of the boundary.

Farrell v. Williams
Hillside Cottage

Mr and Mrs Farrell live in a quiet village in the south west of England. They own a large detached cottage which they purchased in 1998. Their cottage has a long drive of some 50 yards. The driveway is along the western side of the garden and exits West onto Hill Road. Opposite the Farrell's house is Hill Top Cottage owned by Mr and Mrs Williams. Dividing their respective gardens is a line of conifer trees which were planted by Mr and Mrs Farrell in 1999. In 2015, Mr and Mrs Williams who moved in to their property in 2010 propose a new route for vehicles to enter their property. However, the proposed route would mean vehicles crossing what Mr and Mrs Farrell consider to be their garden. Mr and Mrs Williams claim that the trees planted by Mr and Mrs Farrell are on their land and they intend to cut them down. Mr and Mrs Farrell are adamant that the trees should not be cut down.

Rough Sketch from Mr Farrell of the site:

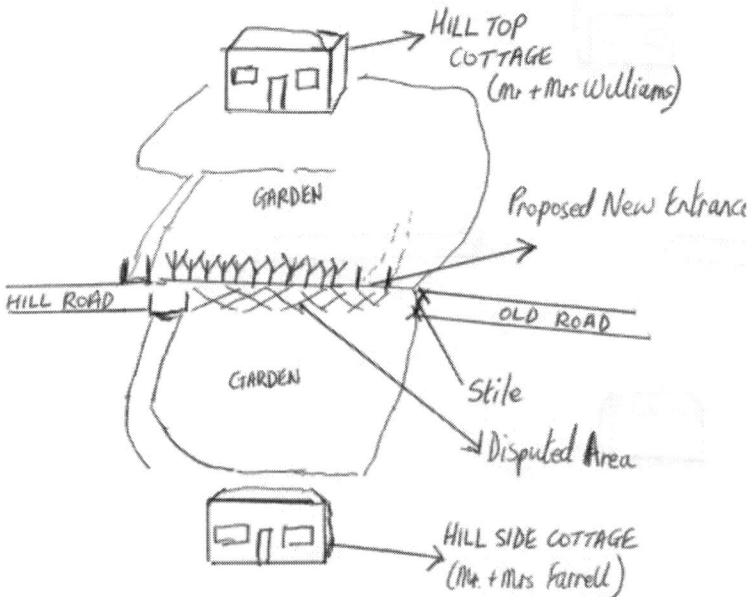

Plan attached to Conveyance for the sale of land on which
Hill Side Cottage stands:

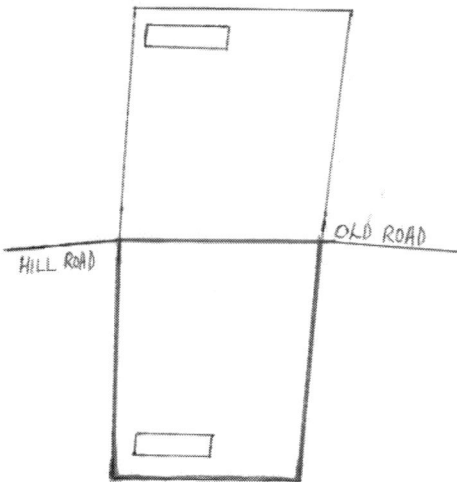

The description in the conveyance which
sold off Hill Cottage

*"All that piece or parcel of land situated south of a line between "Hill
Road" to the West and "Old Road" in the East and for the purposes
of identification shown edged red on the attached plan"*

The wording in the conveyancing suggests we should place
emphasis on the wording and not the attached plan. However, if
the wording of this conveyance is not regarded as totally clear, a
court will look at the plan to see it gives any information which
supplements the wording in the conveyance. The wording in the
conveyance is not totally clear as there could be some doubt as to
how far south does the land stretch and do the east and west
boundaries run perpendicular to the line between Hill Road and
Old Road? The plan does not give much helpful information and
so there will be a need to take into account extrinsic evidence

such as the features on the ground as to the exact position of the line. It is reasonable to assume that Hill Road and Old Road are of a particular width and the description does not say from which point on the two roads the line is drawn. This point can be explained by the looking at the diagram below:

What the description in the conveyance does not make clear is at what points on Hill Road and Old Road does the boundary join up? Obviously, the exact position of the boundary will depend on whether it runs from A to B, C to D or E to F. Therefore, the physical features on the ground may assist in this regard. There might be some boundary posts or other markers on the ground which have been in place since the time the land was first divided. If the land was divided a long time ago, then the chances of the original boundary features being intact are more remote. However, there might be old aerial photographs that show the boundary and may help to determine more precisely the line of the boundary. We do know the width of Hill Road and Old Road at the time. If they were "C" roads then, from Government figures the average width of such a road would be about 6 metres[3], and that would show the difference in the exact boundary depending from what point the line is drawn. If they were old country tracks then of course the width might have been less.

The main thing which the case of Farrell and Williams demonstrates is that it is very difficult to look back and try to determine the precise position of a boundary if it was not clearly done so at

[3] Answer by *Parliamentary Under-Secretary, Department for Transport*, 30 October 2003.

the time the land was divided. If that is the case then it makes you wonder why people will be prepared to spend thousands of pounds on going to court to argue over a few inches of land. Although the title of this book is how to be a litigant in person, that does not mean that litigants in person should not be told in no uncertain terms that there are often much better ways of determining a boundary dispute. Going to court may not be the most appropriate in terms of costs. Parties to a boundary dispute should consider other forms of adjudication. As an expert is often likely to be instructed by the parties if they proceed to court, then why not agree to have the dispute determined by an independent surveyor who specialises in boundary issues? Indeed, this idea is the basis of a Bill that has been put before Parliament by the Earl of Lytton in 2015. The Bill (Property Boundaries (Resolution of Disputes) Bill) will probably not make its way onto the Statute book because the Government believes it would not be appropriate as there are often points of law which it is stated should be decided by lawyers. That might be the case but experienced surveyors who specialise in the field probably have just as good an understanding of the law in the field as some lawyers (or even District Judges) in this area. The proposed Bill has a lot in common with the Party Wall Act 1996.

Boundary disputes undoubtedly create much stress and tension between neighbours and therefore the process of mediation, though often suggested as a method of resolving such disputes, does not seem the most logical way to proceed; neighbours who have dug themselves into entrenched positions are arguably less likely to reach a compromise. In my experience, all that a mediator tends to do is probe the weak points of a case and engage in project fear about the costs if they do not settle. A mediator does not decide the issue but tries to get the parties to come to a settlement (or compromise). It is certainly true the cost of litigation in boundary disputes can escalate to very large figures but, rather than be forced to settle, surely it is better for you to utilise a process that makes a decision on the facts and law.

Why spend £2,000 on a mediation, on the chance that it might reach a fudged compromise, when you could spend the same amount on an independent expert/arbitrator to actually make a decision? The Chartered Institute of Arbitrators has developed costs controlled arbitration schemes which are certainly worth considering.

If you have tried all other methods of resolving a boundary dispute, i.e. have put forward the suggestion of an expert determining the matter or arbitration but that is rejected by the other party, then going to court is the last resort; even then you should not enter into such action lightly.

Help with drafting a boundary claim

Having taken the decision to issue court action, then it is vital to have your claim properly set out. In this respect, you should consider either going to a firm of solicitors who will then probably instruct a barrister to draft the Particulars of Claim or you could see if it is possible to go direct to a barrister under the direct access scheme. Barristers normally only accept instructions from a law firm but some barristers are licenced to receive instructions directly from members of the pubic. Direct access barristers will require payment upfront for the specific task they are being asked to do and it might well be that they will say to the member of the public that it is not appropriate for them to act on a direct access basis. There may be cases where the barrister thinks it is appropriate to have a solicitor instruct the barrister in the normal way because the client is not able to understand the issues or is not capable of providing the barrister with what they need.

The public's perception that the only type of law firms that exist are firms of solicitors is not an accurate picture of what is now starting to happen in the legal market place. Traditionally, solicitors were the only type of law firm that was regulated and permitted to undertake reserved activities such as litigation. The consumer now has a much wider choice of the type of law firm which they can instruct and hence that choice can in some instances lead to them getting the same or a better service at a lower cost. There are three types of "lawyer" who can be regulated to set up in legal practice: Solicitors, Barristers and Chartered Legal Executives. Solicitors are regulated by the Solicitors Regulation Authority, Barristers are Regulated by the Bar Council and Chartered Legal Executives are regulated by CILEx Regulation. Lawyers can decide which of the three Regulators they wish to be regulated by; so you can now have alternative business structures where you may have, for example, a group of solicitors and barristers who might wish to set up in legal practice together and they could decide to obtain Regulation by the SRA or the Bar Council. These alternative business structures can be a mix of lawyers and other professionals such as accountants. A legal practice that has solicitors and barristers together can have the advantage of having litigators and advocates under the same roof.

Another new development is that barristers are now able to be licenced to undertake litigation work. In the past, barristers could only undertake advocacy or drafting court papers and giving advice, but they could not undertake correspondence on behalf of litigants with the other party and the signing off of court documents such as the issuing of proceedings. Now that barristers can obtain from the Bar Council permission to litigate, there are firms of barristers forming legal practices that can now conduct litigation and advocacy. Chartered Legal Executives are now also able to obtain a licence to set up in legal practice on their own or in partnership with others. Often members of the public do not realise that Chartered Legal Executives have the same rights, or can obtain the same rights, as solicitors; they can apply for example to be district judges just as solicitors and barristers can. What this all means to the legal consumer is that there is going to be a greater variety of choice as to who they choose to be represented by and in what manner. It may be that choosing to instruct one of these alternative business structures will prove cheaper because they are often smaller niche practices that have lower overheads.

The particulars of claim in a boundary dispute

The litigant in person ought to have the Particulars of Claim properly drafted by an appropriate lawyer. It is a false economy to do this part of a claim yourself. This book is about being a litigant in person but that does not mean that you should do every stage of the process yourself. In certain types of claim, such as boundary disputes, the particulars should be drafted by someone who knows what they are doing. Therefore, it is worth trying to approach a barrister on a direct access basis to have the court claim properly set out. Barristers are skilled at setting out the wording of a claim and, if this matter were to proceed to a trial, the way the particulars of claim are worded is important. You can almost always agree a fixed fee with a direct access barrister and it would also be useful to ask them to advise on the prospects of success.

Key points in boundary disputes:

- **The Land Registry Title Plans only show general boundary unless the boundary has been specifically determined**
- **To determine a boundary, you need to look at the "parcel clause" of the conveyance which described the property conveyed**
- **If the title deeds give a clear description of the boundary then extrinsic evidence is not considered**
- **If the title deed is not clear, then you can consider external factors**
- **Always consider alternative means of resolving any boundary dispute. Court should always be the last resort. Courts dislike the amount of time and money taken up over sometimes trivial amounts of land. You may not necessarily get your costs even if you win**

your case because the court might consider that there was a reasonable alternative method of resolving the issues.

- **Arbitration or agreeing to be bound by an independent expert report, such as one provided by an experienced boundary surveyor are very sensible alternatives to expensive and time consuming legal action.**

Rights of Way Disputes

Closely linked to boundary disputes are issues concerning rights-of-way. A common dispute that arises is where it is alleged that a right of way has been obstructed. In some instances, the obstruction of a right of way is obvious; a high barbed wire fence going across the whole right of way leaves little room for dispute about its obstruction. However, as in many areas of litigation, things are not always so black-and-white.

Bratton v. Jones

Consider the situation of Ethel Jones and Mr Brian Bratton. Mrs Jones lives in an end terrace house in Upton. There is a lane at the side of her house, 10 St Mary's Place, and a passageway along the back of the terraces. The title deeds to number 10 St Mary's Place describes the right of way as follows:

"Together with the right of the owners or occupiers for the time being of the property hereby conveyed to pass over the said passage 4 feet wide coloured yellow on the said plan for the purpose of going to and returning from the rear of the property hereby conveyed."

The plan overleaf shows the right of way shaded grey. The owner of number 10 (Mrs Jones) has a yard at the back her house and there is a fence positioned at points A to B to C. Mr Bratton, the owner of number 8, alleged that the fence is obstructing the right of way and is threatening to take down the fence. It is true that

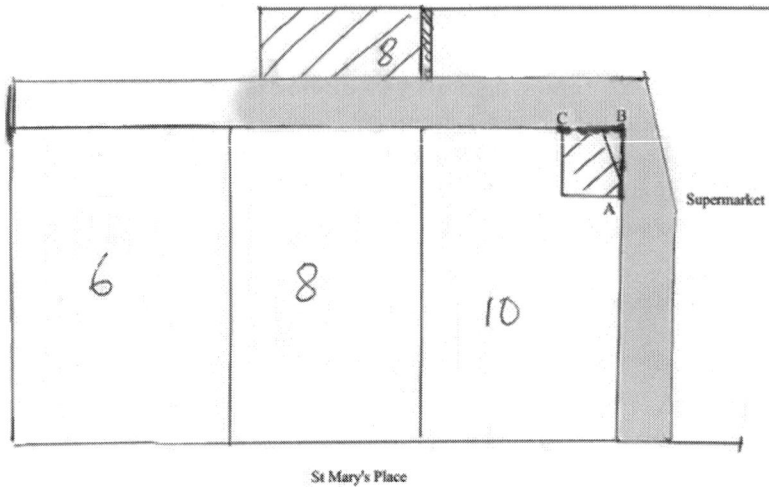

St Mary's Place

the right of way on the corner by the fence is slightly narrower than the rest of the right of way but does that mean that Mr Bratton has a legal action for an interference with the right of way?

The first thing to determine is the nature of the right of way, i.e. is it a right on foot, vehicular or both. Case law suggests that the words granting a right of way are to be given their natural meaning and the words used in the document should be read in light of the surrounding circumstances. In this situation it can be argued that the nature of the right of way, from the wording and circumstances, is that of a right to pass along the area shaded grey on foot.

Having established the nature of the right of way, what is the legal test in deciding if the right of way is being obstructed? Not every interference with a right of way creates a right of action in law. There must be a substantial interference with it. There would be no actionable interference with a right of way if it can be substantially and practically exercised as conveniently after as before the obstruction.

In the example opposite, Mr Bratton would have no action against Ethel Jones for interference with the right of way unless he can establish that there is a real and substantial interference with the enjoyment of the right of way. In this case, although there appears to be a slight narrowing of the right of way at the corner by the fence positioned at points A,B,C, the right of way can still be exercised substantially and practically as had been done before the alleged obstruction.

Let us consider another situation, which is also quite common to rights of way disputes, that of a landowner placing gates across a right of way.

Case study:
Riley v. Mountford

Mr Riley is a resident on the Cherry Lodge Housing Estate and Mr Mountford is the owner of Cherry Manor. There is a right of way over the track (see page 160) to enable the 20 residents on the Cherry Lodge Estate to access the estate. There have always been gates at positions A and F on the track. However, Mr Mountford has recently installed gates at points B, C, D and E. The distance between gates A and B is approx. 60 metres as it is between B and C. The distance between gates C and D is approx. 85 metres and between D and E, 75 metres. All the gates open by means of pressing an electronic button; no key or password is required.

Mr Riley and other residents ask Mr Mountford to remove the gates B, C, D and E as he argues that they are an obstruction because they are substantially interfering with their right of way. Mr Mountford argues that he has installed the additional gates to slow down traffic which cuts through from the main Upton Road in the south to the main road to Downton in the North. The residents argue that what Mr Mountford is really trying to do is prevent the residents of Cherry Lodge Housing Estate from using the track from points E to A and instead making them enter and exit the track from point F in the north near the main road to Downton. Mr Riley brings an action seeking a declaration that the gates installed by Mr Mountford amount to a substantial interference with the right of way.

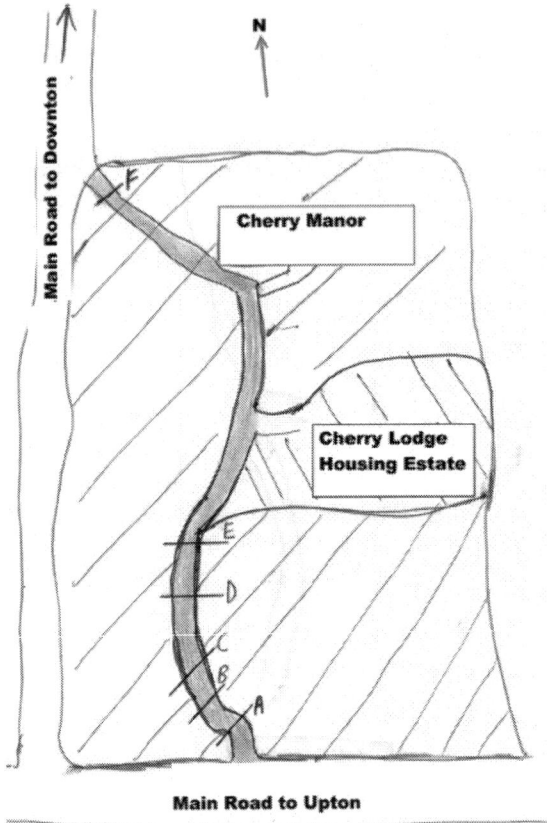

Mr Riley and other residents ask Mr Mountford to remove the gates B, C, D and E as he argues that they are an obstruction because they are substantially interfering with their right of way. Mr Mountford argues that he has installed the additional gates to slow down traffic which cuts through from the main Upton Road in the south *to the main road to Downton in the North. The residents argue that what Mr Mountford is really trying to do is prevent the residents of Cherry Lodge Housing Estate from using the track from points E to A and instead making them enter and exit the track from point F in the north near the main road to Downton. Mr Riley brings an action seeking a declaration that the gates installed by Mr Mountford amount to a substantial interference with the right of way.*

If you put yourself in the shoes of Mr Riley, what are the prospects of him establishing that there is an actionable interference with the right of way? There is a reasonable prospect of arguing that gates B, C, D and E are a substantial interference with the right of way. A person who erects gates over a right of way will not necessarily be obstructing it if the obstacles do not 'substantially interfere' with the right of way. Mr Mountford might argue that he introduced the extra gates, which are operated by a key fob, to slow down the traffic. This has been successfully argued in the case of **Saint v. Jenner (1973)** which involved the installation of speed bumps. However, the recent case of **Kingsgate Development Projects Ltd v. Jordan (2017)** made the point that numerous gates within a short distance may be perceived as an interference even if, when considered in isolation, a single gate might not be. This would be the key point that Mr Riley would be able to raise as the objection to the additional gates at B, C, D and E.

Key points in rights of way disputes

- **Identify the location and the nature of the right of way, i.e. is it for pedestrians only or vehicles as well.**
- **Is there a substantial interference with the right of way**

Access to neighbouring land disputes

Another common situation that arises between neighbours is the inability to agree access so that one neighbour can carry out repairs to their property. It may be that you cannot access your property to carry repairs to your property without trespassing on your neighbour's land. One would have thought that this should be a fairly simple thing to agree and not cause a dispute. However, *"there's nowt so queer as folk"* as the northern saying goes – or words to that effect. Why some landowners take such perverse pleasure in being awkward about neighbours simply wanting to carry our repairs is beyond me. Perhaps it is a manifestation of a personality trait that gives them pleasure in trying to control others? The only reported case on the Access to Neighbouring Land Act 1992 is that of **Prime London Holdings 11 Ltd v. Thurloe Lodge Ltd [2022] EWHC 303 (Ch)** and the judge in that case made a very pertinent observation:

> "If this case has proven anything, it has proven that the Biblical precept to *'love thy neighbour'* is one that owners of neighbouring properties would do well to abide by. The current action has involved great effort and cost to both parties in order to produce an outcome that, with only a modicum of goodwill, they might have been able to agree between them."

But what do you do if the person who lives next to you does not "love thy neighbour" and you need to access their land to repair your property? The first thing to do is take a deep breath and try to avoid confrontation. Start by approaching your neighbours for a friendly conversation about the fact that you need repairs doing to your property. Explain to them what needs doing and why you or your builders need to access their land. It is important to stress that (if it is the case) the works won't cause too much disturbance to them. If they seem agreeable then finish the conversation by saying you will provide them with notice of exactly when your contractors would like access as well as providing them with the contractor's name and insurance details.

If you don't get the consent from your neighbours by way of a simple discussion of the above nature, then you drop them a polite e-mail or letter. The type of initial letter must read as follows:

Dear Mr and Mrs Smith,

Just a short note to say thank you for your time the other night to discuss my need to conduct repairs to my property which would involve going onto your land. You said you were not sure about whether you can agree access. I thought it might be helpful if I set out what exactly needs doing, why I need access to your land and who I intend to get to do the work.

The work required:

The remedial works required are to strip the tiles to enable the rolled lead sheet lining to the valley gutter to be removed and replaced, plus any severely decayed timbers below; the tiles will then be re-installed. The eaves guttering may need to be temporarily removed as well. To undertake this work in a safe manner, access is required to your land in order to erect scaffolding and also to bring in and remove materials. It is estimated that the works would take about 10 days to complete. I attach a plan which shows where the scaffolding would be erected.

Who I propose to instruct to carry the work:

I propose instructing Expert Roofing Repairs Limited of Meadow Lane Upton. They are an established company of some 25 years and they hold public liability insurance of up to £2 million. I have attached a copy of their insurance certificate.

When I would to get the work done:

I would like to get the work done in the middle of August, as that is when they have availability and also it would make sense to do the repairs before this dry summer turns into autumn rain.

I hope the above information is all that you need to be happy to agree access. If you have any more questions, please let me know.

I look forward hearing from you.

Regards

If your neighbour does not allow access then you will need to apply to the court for an Order for Access (N208 claim form). Practice Direction 56 states what information needs to be in the application. Paragraph 11 of the Practice Direction says:

ACCESS TO NEIGHBOURING LAND ACT 1992

11.1 The claimant must use the Part 8 procedure.
11.2 The claim form must set out:
(1) details of the dominant and servient land involved and whether the dominant land includes or consists of residential property;
(2) the work required;
(3) why entry to the servient land is required with plans (if applicable);
(4) the names and addresses of the persons who will carry out the work;
(5) the proposed date when the work will be carried out; and
(6) what (if any) provision has been made by way of insurance in the event of possible injury to persons or damage to property arising out of the proposed work.
11.3 The owner and occupier of the servient land must be defendants to the claim.

The phrase "dominant land" refers to the land of the person making the application. The "servient land" means the land over which you need access to be able carry out the repairs. You should obtain details of the Land Registry Official Copy Entries to illustrate the land involved.

You send the completed N208 Claim Form (along with a copy for the Defendant) to the County Court in the area where your property is. As always, there will be a court fee payable. In this case, the current court fee is £332. The court will send out the Claim Form to your neighbour and they will have 14 days in which to file at court and send the form to the Acknowledgement Service along with any written evidence they wish to rely on. You can, if appropriate, file at court and send to the other party a reply to their written evidence within 14 days. The court is then likely to set a date for a what is called a "disposable hearing" to decide if access should be granted and whether any conditions will be attached to the permission. This disposal hearing will normally be short, lasting no more than an hour.

Key points in a claim for access to neighbouring land:

- **Take all reasonable steps to agree access with your neighbour.**
- **Put down in writing to your neighbour what access you need and why, ensuring the correspondence is kept friendly.**
- **If agreement cannot be reached, then apply to the court for an Order for access.**
- **Remember to include in the Claim Form the items required by practice direction 56.**

❖❖❖

Chapter 9

INHERITANCE CLAIMS

It may seem sad but there is evidence to suggest among lawyers that the number of challenges to wills and claims on estates are on the increase. There are several factors that have probably led to this and not necessarily an increased desire to litigate. Society undergoes changes; the nature of domestic relationships and difficult financial times, such as not being able to put together sufficient money for a deposit on a house, could be issues that mean that when a family member dies some see it as a way of achieving financial security. When the expected inheritance does not appear, then some will want to fight for what they feel is theirs, even if the law does not agree with them.

One of the myths that needs to be dispelled before you make an inheritance claim is that you should never assume that all parties' costs will be paid out of the estate. Making an inheritance claim is adversarial litigation to which the normal costs rules apply that is that the loser pays the winner's costs except in the case of a personal representative who remains neutral.

In recent years there has been a moral debate that has flowed from a decision by the Court of Appeal in the case of **Ilott v. Mitson** which increased an award from £50,000 to £163,000. This was a claim by the daughter of the deceased, who had been out of contact with her mother for many years. The mother made a will which left her out of the estate entirely and her estate went to charities. This decision was seen as an attack on testamentary freedom. The mother and daughter had not been on speaking terms since the daughter left home at the age of 17 and got married to a man whom the mother did not approve of. The daughter fell on hard times and she challenged her mother's will under the Inheritance (Provision for Family and Dependents) Act 1975. The claim was for a failure to provide reasonable financial provision.

The case began a long legal journey in 2004. It eventually ended up with a Judgement in the Supreme Court in March 2017. Under the 1975 act, the daughter was one of a class of people who potentially have a claim if the will does not provide financial provision. There is only one ground for a claim under the Inheritance Act, which is that the disposition (or division) of the deceased's estate, whether following a Will or under the laws of Intestacy, does not make reasonable financial provision for the applicant.

Where the applicant is a spouse, or a civil partner, of the deceased, 'reasonable financial provision' means such provision as would be reasonable in all the circumstances of the case for a husband or wife or a civil partner to receive, whether or not that provision is required for his or her maintenance. The court must consider, but is not bound to follow, the likely settlement that would have been made within divorce proceedings, if the parties had divorced rather than the deceased having died.

For all other applicants under the Inheritance Act, 'reasonable financial provision' means such provision as would be reasonable, given all the circumstances of the case, for the applicant to receive their maintenance. The applicant must show that they had a reasonable expectation of having their living costs met by the deceased. If the applicant was financially independent of the deceased before the date of death, it may be very difficult to show such an expectation.

The case of **Ilott v. Mitson** was heard by the Supreme Court on 12 December 2016. In March 2017, a judgment was delivered which overturned the decision by the Court of Appeal and reinstated that of the judgment given by the District Judge. The Supreme Court decided that the District Judge had in fact weighed up the factors under the 1975 Act correctly. This decision of the highest court in the land was eagerly awaited for guidance in this area of the law and in particular to this controversial area of a claim by an adult child. It probably reinstates the belief that adult children are going to find it difficult to bring a claim unless they are in financial difficulties. It also acknowledged the importance of testamentary freedom. It commented that although a claimant may be entitled to maintenance, it does not mean an entitlement to every type of maintenance.

Following the decision in Mitson, it won't mean a total end to claims by adult children but the court will be more careful in applying the factors it must consider, resulting in the awards to adult children being more modest.

WHO CAN MAKE A CLAIM UNDER THE ACT?

Section 1 of the Act sets out who can make a claim. It reads:

Application for financial provision from deceased's estate.

(1) Where after the commencement of this Act a person dies domiciled in England and Wales and is survived by any of the following persons:—

(a) the spouse or civil partner of the deceased;

(b) a former spouse or former civil partner of the deceased, but not one who has formed a subsequent marriage or civil partnership;

(b a) any person (not being a person included in paragraph (a) or (b) above) to whom subsection (1A) or (1B) below applies;

(c) a child of the deceased;

(d) any person (not being a child of the deceased) who in relation to any marriage or civil partnership to which the deceased was at any time a party, or otherwise in relation to any family in which the deceased at any time stood in the role of a parent, was treated by the deceased as a child of the family;

(e) any person (not being a person included in the foregoing paragraphs of this subsection) who immediately before the death of the deceased was being maintained, either wholly or partly, by the deceased;

that person may apply to the court for an order under section 2 of this Act on the ground that the disposition of the deceased's estate effected by his will or the law relating to intestacy, or the combination of his will and that law, is not such as to make reasonable financial provision for the applicant.

(1A) This subsection applies to a person if the deceased died on or after 1st January 1996 and, during the whole of the period of two years ending immediately before the date when the deceased died, the person was living—

(a) in the same household as the deceased, and

(b) as the husband or wife of the deceased.

(1B) This subsection applies to a person if for the whole of the period of two years ending immediately before the date when the deceased died the person was living—

(a) in the same household as the deceased, and

(b) as the civil partner of the deceased.

*that person may apply to the court for an order under section 2
of this Act on the ground that the disposition of the deceased's
estate effected by his will or the law relating to intestacy, or the
combination of his will and that law, is not such as to make
reasonable financial provision for the applicant.*

WHAT ORDERS CAN BE MADE?

The judge has a wide discretion to redistribute assets to provide a
fair result. The court can make any of the following orders:-

*a) an order that the applicant should receive regular payments
(known as 'periodical payments') from the net estate of the
deceased, for as much and for as long as the judge considers
reasonable.*
*b) an order that the applicant should receive a single lump sum
payment from the estate.*
*c) an order that a property owned by the deceased be
transferred to the applicant.*
*d) an order for the settlement of any property for the benefit of
the applicant i.e.. an order creating a trust for the applicant.*
*e) an order for the purchase of property using assets of the
estate, and for such property either to be transferred to the
applicant or to be held in trust for their benefit.*
*f) an order varying any pre- or post-nuptial (or pre- or post-
civil partnership) settlement to which the deceased was a
party, for the benefit of a surviving spouse or civil partner, or
for a child or step-child of the deceased.*

WHAT FACTORS DO THE COURTS HAVE TO CONSIDER?

In deciding whether to make an order under the Inheritance Act,
the court must first decide whether the Will of the deceased, or the

Laws of Intestacy, make reasonable financial provision for the applicant, and only if such provision has not been made, whether and in what manner it should exercise its powers to make one of the above orders.

The specific factors that the court must consider under section 3(1) of the 1975 Act when deciding these questions are as follows:

1. the financial resources and financial needs which the applicant has or is likely to have in the foreseeable future;
2. the financial resources and financial needs which any other applicant for an order under the Inheritance Act from the estate of the deceased has or is likely to have in the foreseeable future;
3. the financial resources and financial needs which any beneficiary of the estate of the deceased has or is likely to have in the foreseeable future;
4. any obligations and responsibilities which the deceased had towards any applicant for an order or towards any beneficiary of their estate;
5. the size and nature of the net estate of the deceased
6. any physical or mental disability of any applicant or any beneficiary of the estate
7. any other matter, including the conduct of the applicant or any other person, which in the circumstances of the case the court may consider relevant.

A claim under the 1975 act has to be brought within six months of probate. This does not provide a great deal of time in which to assess and prepare a claim. This is further compounded by the fact that under the 1975 act claims are brought under the part eight procedure which requires the written evidence that supports the claim to be filed at court at the time the claim is issued. The example of Ellen Loveridge against the estate of Frank Sampson deceased, analyses and explains what happens in a claim in which a litigant in person may bring a claim under the 1975 act.

Case study:
Frank Sampson and Ellen Loveridge

Frank Sampson died at the age of 65 leaving an estate of nearly £1 million. He left the large bulk of his estate to his children by way of a legacy of £250,000 to Jean and £250,000 to Thomas. The remainder of the estate is left to various charities in many legacies of £20,000 each. His former girlfriend and cohabitee (Ellen Loveridge) was only left a legacy of £5,000. Ellen was very disappointed with this and believes that she should have been left much more, expecting a figure of £250,000 as was left to Jean and Thomas. Ellen considers bringing a claim under the 1975 Act. Ellen is aware that Jean and Thomas have their doubts as to whether Ellen was cohabiting with Frank. The executors to the estate are a firm of solicitors called Vanguard & Co. They had been Frank's lawyers throughout his lifetime.

One aspect of inheritance claims which is not always understood is that the executors should generally take a neutral stance. If they don't take this position the executors run the risk of exposing themselves personally to costs. The role of the executor is to protect the estate. This is why you will notice that the response to a claim from the executors will simply be a factual reply setting out the details of the will, probate and the extent of the estate. Usually there will be no comment on the merits of the claim.

So, putting yourself in the shoes of Ellen Loveridge, what would she have to do as a litigant in person to bring a successful claim under the 1975 act?

The key issue is to provide evidence that Ellen was cohabiting with Frank Sampson in the immediate two years prior to his death. Before 1996, it had been necessary for a cohabitant applying under the Act to show dependency upon the deceased under Section 1(1)(e), but, since the amendments introduced by the Law Reform (Succession) Act 1995, in order to qualify as an applicant, it is necessary to show that he or she had lived with the deceased:

"during the whole of the period of two years ending immediately before the date when the deceased died"

and that the conditions of the cohabitation had been as follows:

(a)in the same household as the deceased and
(b) as the husband or wife of the deceased.

So the important aspects are, What is meant by "the same household" and living together as "husband and wife" or in the case of same sex couples, living together as "civil partners".

THE "SAME HOUSEHOLD"

Ellen could produce evidence of living together in the same household from evidence such as being on the same Council Tax bill and witness evidence. What if Ellen had been keeping her own house and Frank had his own place, and they were splitting the week between the two properties?

The case of **Kotke v. Saffarine [2005]** demonstrates that it is possible for a couple to retain individual properties and still be in the same household. L.J. Ward stated:

> *"will be in the same household if they are tied by their relationship. The tie of that relationship may be made manifest by various elements, not simply their living under the same roof, but the public and private acknowledgment of their mutual society, and the mutual protection and support that binds them together."*

A subsequent case of **Baynes v. Hedger (2008)** said on the subject that at the end of the day, whether two people are living together in the same household is one of fact. Justice Lewison summed this up by saying:

"Statements of general principle such as this must of course be read in the light of the facts of the case. Human relationships are many and various and it is perfectly possible that two people have a long-term, loving and intimate relationship without ever living in the same household; or, having once lived in the same household, decide to live in separate households, while continuing the relationship. In deciding whether two people have lived together in the same household during the whole of the requisite two-year period the court's gaze is not confined to that two-year period, in so far as previous events explain what was happening within that period. Nor, if two people are living in the same household will they necessarily stop doing so merely because they are temporarily physically separated. In the end, it seems to me that the question whether two people live together in the same household is essentially one of fact."

LIVING TOGETHER AS "HUSBAND & WIFE"

The 1975 Act did not intend that every house sharer would qualify under the Act. The relationship must have certain necessary features present if they are to be regarded as living together as husband and wife. This was addressed in *Re Watson (deceased)* [1999] 1 FLR 918. There the applicant had described her relationship as follows: "we were really to the rest of the world man and wife". Mr Justice Neuberger identified this objective feature and adopted the "Clapham Omnibus bystander's"[4] view of the relationship. The court should ask itself the question:

"whether in the opinion of a reasonable person with normal perceptions, it could be said that the two people in question were living together as husband and wife, but when considering that question one should not ignore the multifarious nature of marital relationships."

---

[4] The man on the Clapham Omnibus in a hypothetical ordinary and reasonable person, used by the courts in English law where it is necessary to decide whether a party has acted as a reasonable person would.

In the case of **Churchill v. Roach [2003]** the following features were identified as important to identifying a relationship of living together as "husband and wife":

    (i)   elements of permanence
    (ii) the intimacy of the relationship
    (iii) an element of mutual support
    (iv) consideration of the degree of voluntary restraint upon personal freedom
    (v) an element of community of resources

In the case study of Frank Sampson and Ellen Loveridge, it would assist Ellen's case if she could find witnesses who would be prepared to say that as far as the outside world was concerned, they were together as a couple. That may not be easy. If they were a private couple who did not socialise much then that might cause a problem.

Starting a Claim

A claim under the Inheritance (Provision for Family & Dependents) Act 1975 must be brought before 6 months from the date on which the representation to the estate of the deceased is first taken out. To start a claim, the following needs to be delivered to the court:

1. Claim Form (N208)
2. Written evidence in the form of witness statements
3. The court fee

The Claim can be issued in the Family or Chancery Divisions of the High Court or in the County Court. The County Court has unlimited jurisdiction However, if there are other claims alongside (e.g. validity of wills), or the claim is complex, the High Court may be appropriate.

At the end of this chapter is the Claim Form and an extract of a supporting witness statement from the above case study of **Ellen Loveridge and the Estate of Frank Sampson**. CPR Part 57 and the accompanying Practice Direction 57, contain the rules that govern this type of claim. Before you commence such a claim, you should familiarise yourself with this section of the court rules. It is important to note what the written evidence must contain. The relevant extract from CPR Part 57 is set out below.

> **57.16**
> *(1) A claim under section 1 of the Act must be made by issuing a claim form in accordance with Part 8.*
>
> *(2) Rule 8.3 (acknowledgment of service) and rule 8.5 (filing and serving written evidence) apply as modified by paragraphs (3) to (5) of this rule.*
>
> *(3) The written evidence filed and served by the claimant with the claim form must, except in the circumstances specified in paragraph (3A), have exhibited to it an official copy of –*
>
> *(a) the grant of probate or letters of administration in respect of the deceased's estate; and*
>
> *(b) every testamentary document in respect of which probate or letters of administration were granted.*
>
> *(3A) Where no grant has been obtained, the claimant may make a claim without naming a defendant and may apply for directions as to the representation of the estate. The written evidence must—*
>
> *(a) explain the reasons why it has not been possible for a grant to be obtained;*
>
> *(b) be accompanied by the original or a copy (if either is available) of the will or other testamentary document in respect of which probate or letters of administration are to be granted; and*

(c) contain the following information, so far as known to the claimant—

(i) brief details of the property comprised in the estate, with an approximate estimate of its capital value and any income that is received from it;

(ii) brief details of the liabilities of the estate;

(iii) the names and addresses of the persons who are in possession of the documents relating to the estate; and

(iv) the names of the beneficiaries and their respective interests in the estate.

(3B) Where a claim is made in accordance with paragraph (3A), the court may give directions as to the parties to the claim and as to the representation of the estate either on the claimant's application or on its own initiative.

(Section 4 of the 1975 Act as amended confirms that nothing prevents the making of an application under the Act before representation with respect to the estate of the deceased person is taken out.)

(4) Subject to paragraph (4A), the time within which a defendant must file and serve –

(a) an acknowledgment of service; and

(b) any written evidence,

is not more than 21 days after service of the claim form on him.

Settling an inheritance claim

It is very probable that a claim under the 1975 Act will be settled long before it reaches the courtroom. Of course, attempts to settle this kind of dispute should be encouraged; a dispute of this nature often brings to the forefront a lot of pent up family emotions over perceived unfairness of the Will. This obviously affects objectivity when considering what is a reasonable settlement figure. The process of weighing up all the factors that have to be considered and reaching a figure may seem like a judge is plucking numbers out of the air but what should be remembered is that it is very difficult to arrive at a figure that reflects reasonable financial provision. If the judge has applied his mind to all of the relevant factors then it would be difficult to appeal the decision the judge arrives at. This uncertainty should encourage a claimant in such a case to be open to reasonable proposals.

In the case of a claim by a spouse, most of the cases revolve around what the award should be. The court as in all inheritance claims under the Act applies the factors in section 3(1). The clearest guide as to the level of provision is the so called "divorce test". The court is likely to be at least as generous to the widow or widower as it would have been to a former spouse claiming financial provision following a divorce. What should be remembered though is this test does not mean that a "divorce type" calculation should be seen as the ceiling to an award or the minimum amount.

The case of **Ellen Loveridge and the Estate of Frank Sampson**, is a claim by a cohabitee for reasonable financial maintenance, which is not the same as reasonable financial provision in the case of a spouse. The Supreme Court in the case of **Illot v. Mitson (2017)** gave useful guidance as to the meaning of "maintenance". It stated:

> The matters to which the court must have regard in exercising its power to award reasonable financial provision are listed under s.3 of the Act. For an applicant other than a spouse or partner, reasonable financial provision is limited to what it would be reasonable for her to receive for maintenance only. This is an objective standard, to be determined by the court. The limitation to maintenance provision represents a deliberate legislative choice and demonstrates the significance attached by English law to testamentary freedom. Maintenance cannot extend to any or everything which it would be desirable for the claimant to have, but is not limited to subsistence level. The level at which maintenance may be provided is clearly flexible and falls to be assessed on the facts of each case, as at the date of hearing. Although maintenance is by definition the provision of income rather than capital, it may be provided by way of a lump sum. **[12-25]**

The passage on the previous page recognises the importance of testamentary freedom and that the amount of the award for maintenance would not necessarily mean everything which the applicant would regard as desirable to have nor so low as to be merely subsistence.

It is quite likely that a court would award a capital sum to Ellen Loveridge but would that capital be greater than the £5,000 she was left in the Will? There is a very good prospect that Ellen would receive more than £5,000. In her case, the key factors to consider are:

- Her current financial needs and for the foreseeable future
- Her current earnings (£800 per month)
- Her age (58) and future earning capacity
- The size of the estate (£900,000)
- The needs of other beneficiaries
- The length of the time they had cohabited
- Intention to get married

Whilst not wanting to put an exact figure on what a judge might award in this situation, it is not inconceivable that Ellen could expect £150,000 from the estate.

Costs in an inheritance claim

The general rule in respect of costs applies in claims brought under the 1975 Act. The unsuccessful party will usually be ordered to pay the costs of the successful party. However, the court has discretion to depart from this rule in certain circumstances and may order the costs to be paid from the deceased's estate, each party to pay their own costs or in unusual cases order the winner to pay the loser's costs. The winner might be ordered to pay the loser's costs where they have acted in a particularly deceitful or aggressive manner or have refused Alternative Dispute Resolution such as mediation.

	Claim Form	**In the** IN THE COUNTY COURT at UPTON	
	(CPR Part 8)	**Claim no.**	A20UP999
		Fee Account no.	
		Help with Fees - **Ref no.** (if appli-cable)	H W F – ☐☐☐ – ☐☐☐

Claimant

Ms Ellen Loveridge
19 Ferndale Road
UPTON
UP1 9TH

(SEAL)

Defendant(s)

1) Fred Finch (as executor of the estate of Mr Frank Sampson [Deceased])
2) Jean Sampson
3) Thomas Sampson
4) Upton Dogs Home (Registered Charity No. 999999)

Does your claim include any issues under the Human Rights Act 1998? ☐ Yes ☑ No

Details of claim (see also overleaf)

Details of claim (see also overleaf)

1. The Claimant, who was born on 10 June 1963, is a person entitled under section 1AThe Inheritance (Provision for Family and Dependants) Act 1975 (the "Act") to seek an order under section 2 of the Act.
2. The deceased died on 13 November 2020 domiciled in England and Wales.
3. Probate of the last will of the deceased dated 16 June 2006 was granted to the First Defendant on 3 January 2021.
4. The value of the net estate from the grant appears to be a sum not exceeding £900,000. Under the will the Claimant received a gift of £5,000. The Claimant seeks the following relief:

a) Reasonable financial provision out of the net estate of Mr Frank Sampson ('the Deceased'), under the Inheritance (Provision for Family and Dependants) Act 1975;
b) Provision for the costs of this claim to be paid out of the Deceased's net estate.
c) Such further or other relief as the Court thinks just.

Further details of the Claimant's claim are set out in her witness statement a copy of which is served herewith. The procedure in CPR Part 8 applies to this Claim.

Defendant's name and address	Fred Finch (Executor of Frank Sampson Deceased) Vinegar Finch & Co Church Street UPTON UP9 2HU		£
		Court fee	332
		Legal representative's costs	
		Issue date	1 May 2023

For further details of the courts www.gov.uk/find-court-tribunal.
When corresponding with the Court, please address forms or letters to the Manager and always quote the claim number.

N208 Claim form (CPR Part 8) (10.20) © Crown copyright 2020

Claim no.	A20UP999

Details of claim (continued)

Claimant's or claimant's legal representative's address to which documents should be sent if different from overleaf. If you are prepared to accept service by DX, fax or e-mail, please add details.

Statement of Truth

I understand that proceedings for contempt of court may be brought against anyone who makes, or causes to be made, a false statement in a document verified by a statement of truth without an honest belief in its truth.

☑ **I believe** that the facts stated in these particulars of claim are true.

☐ **The Claimant believes** that the facts stated in these particulars of claim are true. **I am authorised** by the claimant to sign this statement.

Signature

Ellen Loveridge

☑ Claimant

☐ Litigation friend (where claimant is a child or a Protected Party)

☐ Claimant's legal representative (as defined by CPR 2.3(1))

Date

Day	Month	Year
30	04	2023

Full name

ELLEN LOVERIDGE

Name of claimant's legal representative's firm

If signing on behalf of firm or company give position or office held

Find out how HM Courts and Tribunals Service uses personal information you give them when you fill in a form: https://www.gov.uk/government/organisations/hm-courts-and-tribunals-service/about/personal-information-charter

IN THE COUNTY COURT at UPTON

CHANCERY BUSINESS

IN THE MATTER OF THE INHERITANCE (PROVISION FOR FAMILY

AND DEPENDANTS) ACT 1975

BETWEEN:

ELLEN LOVERIDGE

Claimant

-and-

(1)   FRED FINCH

(as executor of the estate of FRANK SAMPSON - Deceased)

(2)   JEAN SAMPSON

(3)   THOMAS SAMPSON

(4)   UPTON DOGS HOME (Registered Charity No. 999999)

Defendants

————————————————--

WITNESS STATEMENT OF ELLEN LOVERIDGE

————————————————

I, ELLEN LOVERIDGE, of 19 Ferndale Road, UPTON, UP1 9TH, do state as follows:

1.   I am the Claimant in these proceedings. I make this statement in support of my claim for reasonable financial provision out of the estate of Mr Frank Sampson, under the Inheritance (Provision for Family and Dependants) Act 1975. I bring the claim because during the whole of the two-year period ending immediately before the date when the deceased died, I was living in the same household as the deceased and living as the wife of the deceased. My date of birth is 10.06.1963.

2.   In this statement, I refer to a Bundle of documents marked "EL", (hereafter the "Bundle").

3.   My partner, Frank Sampson, died on 13 November 2020, aged 65. He left a will dated 16 June 2006. A copy of that will is attached at **pages 1 to 3** of the Bundle. The effect of that will is that he appointed the partners in Vanguard & Co Solicitors as his executors and trustees. He gave £250,00 to his sister Jean Sampson, £250,000 to his brother Thomas Sampson; I received £5,000. The residuary estate was left to various charities in amounts of £20,000

4.   Probate of the will was granted to the First Defendant, Mr Fred Finch, who I understand to be a partner in Vanguard & Co Solicitors, on 3 January 2017. A copy of the grant of probate is at **page 4** of the Bundle.

5.   I stand to receive only £5,000. I first met Frank in 2001 and in 2002 we moved in together. Although his last Will of 16 June 2006 only left me the £5,000, we had discussed this a few months before he died and in fact he had made an appointment only the week before he died to see his solicitor on 2 October 2020 to update his Will. I refer to a copy of a letter from Vanguard & Co confirming the appointment at **page 8** of the Bundle. Another reason why we had been discussing the updating of the Will was that we had been discussing plans to get married in the summer of 2019. In the Bundle at **pages 9 to 12** are copies of details from several venues we were thinking of booking for the wedding.

6.   We lived at his home at 18 Ferguson Close, Upton. I had been living at 25 Grove Road, Upton, with my daughter Jody. Once I moved in with Frank, I only spent occasional days at the property My daughter Jody continues to live at that property and recently her boyfriend has moved into the property with her. I moved in with Frank as I said in 2002 and it can be shown

that from that year Frank had contacted the local council to say that he was no longer entitled to a single person discount on his Council Tax bill as I was living with him. A copy of the Council Tax for that year showing the removal of the single person discount is at **page 9** of the Bundle.

7. After I moved in with Frank, he encouraged me to reduce my working hours from full time down to 12 hours as he had sufficient monies to maintain a good standard of living on his earnings alone. The house we lived in at 18 Ferguson Close is a 5 bedroom detached house with a stable block and extensive gardens amounting to one acre. We took regular foreign holidays each year and travelled to Australia and Canada. It was apparent to those who knew us that we were living together as husband and wife; although we did not have a large circle of friends, we clearly were a couple.

8. Now that Frank has died, I am in difficult financial circumstances. The property (18 Ferguson Close) was in Frank's sole name and is to be sold. The executors and Frank's son and daughter have asked me to leave the property even before it is sold. I am currently staying temporarily with a friend but I am only allowed to stay for a few months until I find somewhere else to live. I have been looking to rent a one-bedroom flat in Upton and the lowest rent I have found is £700 per month. I would also need to put down a deposit and pay one month's rent in advance. I currently only work 12 hours per week at the Post Office in Upton earning £800 per month net. Clearly on this salary I could not afford to rent a property. When I moved in with Frank, I reduced the hours I worked from full time to the current 12 hours. I have considered finding employment with more hours but at my age this is going to be difficult. I only have £1,500 in savings at this current time as I have used up much of my savings to cover living expenses.

Chapter 10

Can the Litigant in Person Claim Costs?

The costs of a litigant in person are as a result of statute. No right existed under common law. The Litigants in Person (Costs and Expenses) Act 1975 (as amended) gives the LIP the right to recover 'sums in respect of any work done, and any expenses and losses incurred, by the litigant in or in connection with the proceedings to which the order relates'.

A LIP seeking to claim costs may present a claim calculated in one of two ways:

As of 2017, the hourly rate which can be claimed by a litigant in person (who cannot prove actual financial loss) is £19 for time spent on their cases. In respect of either category, the maximum the LIP can recover for time is two-thirds of the amount that would have been allowed if legally represented. This limit does not apply to disbursements. The reason for applying this cap is that a solicitor's charges have usually included a profit mark-up on his expense rate, but as a LIP they may not make a profit out of the costs of litigation. The mark up is deducted, leaving two-thirds. Since there is no profit mark-up on disbursements, the two-thirds rule does not apply to them.

In respect of financial loss, the litigant in person is required to establish by evidence. The case of **Joseph v. Boyd & Hutchinson [2003] EWHC 413** gave some guidance as to defining whether a financial loss had been suffered by a LIP. It was said that the court should:

> *"adopt a 'broad brush' approach and not enquire to any great extent whether the 'Litigant in Person' would have been engaged on other business. If he was available during working hours, one can assume he was available to work. However, even if one adopts such an approach, the Litigant in Person' must nevertheless go on to show that he would have been gainfully employed and, more importantly, how much he would have earned. It is the amount lost that gives rise to the claim for financial loss. In practice, it is often on this last limb that litigants in person fail."*

It is because of the difficulty of showing the financial loss that a litigant in person's costs will usually be stated according to the hourly rate of £19.

If the litigant in person seeks costs, he should file and serve written evidence to show actual loss at least 24 hours prior to any hearing so that the court will have time to consider the costs.

❖❖❖

Conclusion

It is hoped that this book has provided practical guidance to a litigant in person. It should be clear that the legal world is changing with an increasing number of people conducting court action without legal representation. This trend has arisen for a number of reasons and the courts are recognising that more people are acting for themselves. Lawyers have been given new professional guidance about how to deal with litigants in person.

Although there is a greater number of litigants in person, that does not mean that they can ignore basic principles of law and procedure. The courts will explain to litigants in person what they need to do but they cannot expect the courts to apply the rules more leniently. Before embarking on any type of court action, it is essential to have undertaken proper preparation so that you set out your case correctly the first time. If you make mistakes it can be difficult and costly to make amendments, so getting it right the first time is vital. The key to a court action is to have an understanding of:

1. The facts of the case,
2. The applicable law, and
3. The court rules.

Even with a small claim it is important to understand the relevant law. The procedure in a small claim is less formal but if you have misapplied the law then you are unlikely to succeed. In larger cases outside of the small claims track, the procedure becomes more formal and contains a lot more steps before arriving at a trial. Although it is difficult for many people to afford legal representation throughout a court case, it would be money well spent to have at least obtained some general advice about your proposed claim before you embark on court action. The key aspect of having independent legal advice before you start court action is that the lawyer will be objective and play the "devil's advocate role". This is a valuable exercise to go through because the biggest criticism of litigants in person is that they struggle to be objective. It is very easy to have tunnel vision when you conduct your own legal case and so having someone to probe the strength of your case is very useful.

If, after having considered the law, you come to a conclusion that you have a reasonable prospect of success, you then have to navigate the court rules. You must comply with deadlines and directions set by the court. A failure to comply can lead to your case being struck out. It may seem wholly unjust for your case to end this way but unfortunately that is the reality of the civil court system. The court system simply does not have enough resources to give litigants several chances to get things done.

Knowing how to negotiate your way around the court rules and to use them to your advantage is part of the litigation process. Litigation in this respect is a bit like a game of chess where you can manoeuvre yourself into a stronger position by making best use of the court rules. Of course a very weak case on the facts and the law is unlikely to succeed, but if you present your case in the best possible light and use the court rules to your advantage, where appropriate, you can increase your chances of success.

If you do not settle your case after going through all the pre-trial stages, you will eventually arrive at the trial. Remember that the trial is your only opportunity to make the right impression with the judge. You should prepare carefully what you intend to say; your arguments should not be an emotional plea to find in your favour but instead a clear and concise presentation of your evidence and appropriate questioning of the witnesses for the other side. Your closing speech should summarise the key points of your case and address any weaknesses exposed by the other side.

Following the guidance in this book will not guarantee success as a litigant in person, but hopefully you will avoid mistakes and present your case in the best possible light.

❖❖❖

Index

❖❖❖